The
Psychology of
LUCK

The Psychology of
LUCK

Korean Secrets for Attracting
Wealth and Success

Min Ji Yoo

Translated by Jinmyung Lee

LEAP

First published in the UK in 2026 by LEAP
An imprint of Bonnier Books UK
5th Floor, HYLO, 105 Bunhill Row,
London, EC1Y 8LZ

A CIP catalogue record for this book is available from the British Library.

Hardback ISBN: 978-1-78512-659-8
Trade Paperback ISBN: 978-1-78512-660-4

Also available as an ebook and an audiobook

1 3 5 7 9 10 8 6 4 2

Design and Typeset by Angie Boutin
Printed and bound in Great Britain by CPI (UK) Ltd, Croydon CR0 4YY

At Bonnier Books UK, we are committed to publishing sustainably.
Find out more here: bonnierbooks.co.uk/sustainability

The authorised representative in the EEA is
Bonnier Books UK (Ireland) Limited.
Registered office address:
Block B, The Crescent Building
Northwood, Santry
Dublin 9, D09 C6X8, Ireland
compliance@bonnierbooks.ie

www.bonnierbooks.co.uk

The Psychology of Luck is an introduction to the mysterious and powerful world of luck as it is understood and practiced in Korea. In this book, Min Ji Yoo explores how luck plays out in our lives and how—with the right approaches and tools—you can harness the power of luck in your own life to attract riches in all their forms.

This translation of the original Korean text has been adapted and edited slightly in order to make the concepts more readily understood for a non-Korean audience.

CONTENTS

The
Psychology of
LUCK

No Wealthy Person Dismisses Luck

In the world of television broadcasting, the forces of luck and fortune are always at work; a single vote can make or break a career. I was able to realize this early on in my career, when I was working on a trot[*] idol singing show that had gripped Korea. The participants, who usually performed for television from markets and event halls across the country, nervously awaited their turn. They had taken part in this challenge hoping to become the "next big star" in trot. If their hopes came

---

[*] Trot is a type of popular Korean music that emerged under the Japanese occupation (1910–1945). Its name comes from "fox trot," although the two-beat rhythm is the only similarity between the two genres. After a period of decline, trot has been regaining popularity among the South Korean audience. Winners of trot idol shows often go on to very successful and lucrative singing careers and can become rich celebrities.

true, they would be able to keep singing and even make a living with their passion. In a sense, the contest was their second chance at a fierce battle they had not been able to win earlier in their lives.

"That one's next!"

The audience assessed the final candidates. To my eye, one candidate was clearly a strong enough singer and performer to make his own destiny, regardless of whether he won the vote count. In the end, that candidate did win the trophy. I had noticed him from the beginning, felt sure he would do very well, and had often shared this sentiment with my colleagues.

When I first started working as a TV producer, my colleagues often told me that I had exceptional intuition. I seemed to know the potential of an idol making their debut after a single meeting. I spotted and cast talented people long before they became known to a popular audience. From the director of photography to the show's writers, people would say to each other about me, "You've got to admit, she's got extraordinary intuition," or "Maybe she can see the future or something." What they were trying to describe was an intuition that would hit me instantly when I laid eyes on someone, an instinct that was almost primal in its simplicity and directness.

This intuition about someone's future was something I had been aware of my whole life, ever since I was a child. The ability to read fortunes ran in my family.

Introduction

In the olden days, there were Il-gwans[*] (astromancers) and Ji-gwans[†] (geomancers) in government positions. An astromancer employs knowledge of traditional astrology and fortune-telling to advise on auspicious dates. As for geomancers, people sought their services to find suitable land for such things as the best site to build a house or situate a grave. People considered them, and fortune-tellers in general, as the spiritual leaders of their town. The three magi who followed the star of Bethlehem were respected astrologers and astronomers. They would also predict a country's future by interpreting the constellations' celestial messages. Very few people were equipped to hold those positions, as they required many years of training and study.

My family has a secret that nobody talks about. We would often have prescient dreams; my father, my older brother, and me. It was all because of my paternal grandmother. There were times when my grandmother would read people's fortunes

---

[*] An Il (day) gwan (official) is a profession that dates back to the Three Kingdoms period (57 B.C.E.–935 C.E.). Il-gwans were in charge of observing celestial bodies to foretell the fortunes of the nation, managing the water clock to provide accurate information regarding time and the weather, maintaining a calendar to help with agricultural planning, etc.

[†] Ji (land) gwans (officials) were experts in feng shui hired by the government to assess land and its fortune based on the theories of yin/yang and the Five Energies and to select and manage the location of major national sites such as royal tombs, palaces, local government offices, etc.

through dreams or mumble to herself nonstop as if a dam had burst.

As I will show you in this book, examining one's "luck," which is invisible, is one of the oldest professions in the history of humanity. Examining and explaining the basis of such an intangible practice is a tricky business. Nevertheless, working in broadcasting, where I witnessed people's worth fluctuate by millions overnight, confirmed my belief in luck. After I left broadcasting and dedicated myself entirely to studying luck, I learned another lesson: "Luck" and "money" are as inseparable as "fish" are from "water." A person who values luck is never poor. Likewise, a person who dismisses luck is never rich. Of course, there were a few exceptions, but this was my observation after working with many people and seeing their luck over time.

This is why I tell people to believe in luck. Luck is useless to those who don't believe in it. Only irrational faith allows you to understand something irrational, for luck is invisible to the ordinary individual. If you want to have better luck or maximize it for your benefit, you first have to believe in it.

In fact, you don't even need to believe in luck. You can start by being mindful of it. This will allow you to use your will to build your luck and keep it for longer when it enters your life. By being aware of luck in your life, you can improve your current situation and build great wealth, whether it be money, love, worldly success, or all three. Luck begets luck. If you study it and value it, you will attract more of it. If you dismiss it or treat it poorly, it will run away from you.

Having now studied luck in my own life and in the lives of many others, I have reached a point where I can assess my personal luck, and that of others, much more realistically. I now understand that there is no such thing as a miracle from the heavens when it comes to luck. I use that knowledge, my intuition, my diverse life experience, and my instinctual sense for what essential insights I must convey to each of my clients to help them understand how the secrets of luck and fate attract wealth and success.

What my work has revealed to me is the surprising discovery that you can become wealthy and successful in any area of your life by adjusting your attitude and mindset toward luck. No wealthy person ignores luck. This book will explain the secrets of attracting wealth and using luck correctly through the stories of some of the people with whom I have worked or studied, including both regular people and some of Korea's wealthiest and most celebrated people. Their lives can dramatically illustrate the ways in which the psychology of luck can play out in all of our lives.

The Psychology of
CERTAINTY

1

The Hidden Secrets of Wealth and Fate

LUCK IS AN ACTIVE FORCE IN THE WORLD

"Apparently they're getting paid one hundred thousand dollars per episode. One hundred thousand dollars!"

"I know. Who could have known they'd become so famous?"

"Jeez. They're so lucky."

The broadcasting company I worked at recently produced a drama series in which a major celebrity had been cast in the lead role. As soon as they were cast, rumors about the actor and how much they were being paid raced through the corridors.

I, an ordinary worker on a company payroll, couldn't even wrap my head around how much money it was. One hundred thousand dollars for each episode? Seriously? A junior producer like myself, who spent more nights at work than at home, could only dream of a paycheck so large.

To be honest, I actually wasn't that surprised, even though my colleagues were. The disparities in wealth in the entertainment business in Korea are extreme. On one side are the well-paid celebrities living their busy, glamorous lives. On the other are collaborators behind the scenes putting our blood, sweat, and tears into creating the glamorous shows that pay the celebrities so well. Our lives are as different as chalk and cheese.

I shrugged and told myself to focus on my own life. Nevertheless, the conversation I had overheard in the corridor stirred a thought that had buried itself deep in my subconscious.

———•———

I was twenty-seven when I started working in television broadcasting. I was put in charge of a show as soon as I joined the company. I was extremely fortunate to be given a show of my own, which usually requires a decade of experience. Directing celebrities, managers, stylists, camera operators, writers, and dozens of other staff was a lot of responsibility for a novice. Landing that job had not been easy, so when I won the position against strong competition, I was publicly congratulated and my profile rose.

But as with any other job, this one had a less-appealing

side, too. I was so busy with my new job that I was unable to go home for days on end. I often had to give up my weekends, too. I was a hamster on its wheel. In this one aspect, the life of a producer is no different from a celebrity's: We are both entirely dependent on the show's schedule.

At first, everything was new and interesting. I was eager to learn and excited to make my debut as a producer. I felt a surge of willpower and energy that made me think I could achieve anything. I ended up doing the job pretty well and accomplished a lot. But after a year, I started to feel both frustration and a new kind of craving growing inside me. What was the reason? Both celebrities and producers work tirelessly under the hot lights, but what separated us most obviously was one thing: money.

Although we were both breaking our backs on the same soundstages, the celebrities were taking home vastly more money than those of us working behind the scenes. I understand that some people may consider this a childish complaint. After all, broadcasting companies are a workplace like any other, and producers are only employees. Some might say, "If you wanted to be rich, why didn't you start your own business instead of working for other people?" But starting your own business is a big risk: A thousand-dollar investment may result in complete failure for one person, while another may collect a hundred times their initial investment. Why?

Working in entertainment, I witnessed firsthand the unpredictable forces of wealth, success, and fate. I heard about

Andrew, a K-pop idol who bought land in one of the most expensive parts of Gangnam, or Eva, an actor who purchased a luxury apartment in a multipurpose building with a view of the Han River. They were all my age and sometimes even younger than I was. Their wealth and success gave me something to ponder:

How did Andrew manage to make so much money so fast?

I haven't even seen Eva that much lately. How did she become so rich?

With all that money, they can stop working right now and still be comfortable, can't they?

I started paying attention to the way they spoke, their attitudes, their habits, their life patterns. I thought that if I observed them hard enough, I could figure out what they did that was fundamentally different from other people, what had brought them all that wealth. Maybe they made their fortunes thanks to some highly valuable, secret information. Maybe they had a hot tip or technique for investing. My brain was obsessed, looking for a simple answer I could put into practice.

But I couldn't find a simple answer. They were them; I was me. They slept as little as I did and were as dedicated as I was. Clearly, they were making better use of their time outside work.

In the end, the celebrities who get one hundred thousand dollars for an episode of dramatic television and the producers who make a pittance are both just hardworking people making the best of their day-to-day lives. Maybe I hadn't looked deeply enough, but I couldn't find any striking difference separating the haves and the have-nots. Even as I reached that conclusion, the conversation I had heard in the corridor came back to me like an echo.

"They're so lucky . . ."

Yes, luck! That was it! I was sure of it. Luck was the reason some people got so much more out of the same amount of effort and dedication. In the world of capitalism, where the stakes are so high, luck must count for more than effort or competence. It must be the key that unlocks million-dollar paychecks and expensive houses.

Working in entertainment, I'd been constantly exposed to people making it big overnight while others failed and went flat broke. Seeing this can't help but make even the most skeptical, rational person rethink their stance on luck. Some force I could not see must have caused two aspiring K-pop idols who debuted at the same time to have dramatically different career paths, turning only one of the rookies into a star after their first appearance on the screen. I began to see that there must be no other explanation for this than luck.

In the entertainment world, a comedian can go from loitering around the lobby of entertainment companies looking for work to seeing his worth skyrocket, with shows fighting over him. I was equally likely to see a celebrated singer suddenly ostracized after they got pulled into a scandal. In this world, it is possible to experience life's extremes, the cold season and the hot season, the best and the worst. As the producer of an idol show, I witnessed these dramatic changes of fate up close.

A contestant who was rather low-key in their performances nonetheless saw their fan base grow week after week. Another contestant, who everyone thought would be the final winner, fell into oblivion after a small mistake got them kicked off the show. If one candidate's performance became a sensation one week, it could eclipse another's, no matter how talented that candidate was. The contest was a battlefield where every day was filled with surprises. It was impossible to guess what would happen next. As I watched the show and the contestants evolved week by week, I began to wonder to myself: *Are skills the only factor that determine a candidate's fate? Or is it fair to assume that those who make it to the finals have made more of an effort than those who were eliminated?* I was sure that among those who had been eliminated, there must have been some contestants who were more talented and more dedicated. Talent wasn't everything, but neither was luck. That's what reality has shown me.

Life truly is about timing. Being talented is not enough. You have to be born in an era when your talent and value are recognized!

———•———

While working on the reality show, I found myself thinking more deeply about the subject of luck. Unexpectedly, pondering it made me feel much more peaceful. Even though the universe of luck is invisible, to me it is somehow easier to understand than the often arbitrary, difficult circumstances of physical existence. I felt as though the thick fog had been lifted.

As my interest in understanding luck grew, I stopped ruminating about why I wasn't making a lot of money and began to ask different questions:

Am I ignorant about the power of luck?

Is luck selective about the people it chooses?

I couldn't help but wonder what secrets of luck the wealthy shared. For some people, luck is a given, but for others, it is something they desperately desire. While you might say that anybody can be lucky, it also seems clear to me that some people never are.

What attracts good luck and increases one's wealth? What is the quickest way to transform one's fate into that of a rich person's? I was impatient to know, but I didn't need to wait for long. Pandora's box opened easily, when I was least expecting it.

"YOU WILL GROW YOUR FORTUNE"

"Someday, you will grow your fortune.
Then you will grow it even more."

The baby's eyes twinkled like glass beads, hinting at all the facets of life to come. The family elder whispered those words about the baby's fortune as she held her enveloped in a blanket. At the time, no one understood what she meant.

My grandmother was endowed with what people might call "exceptional insight." Her knowledge of saju[*] and face-reading[†] was well-known among the town residents, who routinely consulted her on various family matters. They would come to her for advice, and when some unexpected statement

---

[*] Saju represents the year, month, date, and time of one's birth: the "four (sa) pillars (ju)" of fate that saju practitioners analyze to study someone's life. It might be likened to the Western concept of a person's astrological sign and birth chart, determined by the details of their birth.

[†] Gwan (see) sang (shape, appearance) is face-reading, or the art of figuring out someone's temperament, personality, and/or fortune from the way they look.

of hers aligned with the events of their lives, they saw it as a kind of prophecy. They expressed their gratitude and went back to their daily lives with increased dedication.

In her time, my grandmother and others like her could not be open about their gift. Although her importance to the other residents of the town was never formally recognized, her presence was comparable to that of an ancient tree watching over the town. My grandmother was particularly interested in the fortunes of human life: What brought good luck or bad luck? What brought blessings or adversities? What kind of life drew abundance and serenity? She was always interested in those sorts of questions and watched how they played out in her neighbors' lives, advising when she was asked and often giving very valuable advice.

My mother thought my grandmother just had better hunches than the average person. She wasn't interested in knowing why my grandmother would rush out the door when she heard the village drums or what she told the villagers when they sought her out. My mother obstinately tried to rationalize everything. Even when my grandmother mentioned something that came true the very next day, my mother attributed it to my grandmother having lived long enough to make accurate guesses even without concrete, rational information.

My grandmother's attitude changed after I arrived. As the years went by and I grew up, I became increasingly curious about my fate. I would ask my grandmother about it, and she would respond with a gentle reprimand: "That's enough. It's no use learning too much too early. There is a natural order and a right time for everything. I will only tell you this: You will grow your fortune."

I listened to her without saying anything, wondering what she meant.

———

My grandmother passed away when I was in middle school. Following her death, I started having clairvoyant dreams; I had inherited some of her gifts, even if I didn't understand them yet. The apple hadn't fallen far from the tree.

There was a lot I wanted to experience and learn. I became quite perceptive in watching people. That wasn't all. I also became fascinated by the real-life issues that made the world go round. When other kids my age were wondering what job they would have when they grew up or what kind of person they would marry, I was asking myself questions that had nothing to do with my present situation.

"What do you want to be when you're older?"

"I want to be rich. I'm going to make a lot of money."

"Why?"

"Because. I want to be really wealthy."

"How are you going to manage that?"

"Well, I'm not sure, but somehow, I've got to be successful. My grandmother told me so. I'm going to grow my fortune."

I wanted to succeed and fill my pockets with money.

My impatience and curiosity drove me to the outside world. I started a fashion business and then a café. By the time I was in college, I had a monthly income of several thousand dollars, which allowed me to put aside some money. While my friends busied themselves studying and building their résumés for the job market, my focus was entirely on making even more money with the money I already had.

———

It took me exactly thirteen years. Thirteen years to become the owner of a spacious mansion worth six million dollars in Pyeongchang-dong, at the foot of Bukhan Mountain. People ask me how I came to live in such a luxurious residence. Every time I hear such questions, I just smile and say, without hesitation: "I was lucky."

Just like the valedictorian who says they focused on what they learned during class without revealing how much after-school tutoring and studying they also did, most successful people will give you a similar answer and say they owe it all to luck. A person who doesn't believe in luck would probably say, "I see," and not think twice about it. A person who is usually mindful of luck and firmly believes in it would want to know what that person did to be so lucky. If my friend and I both put in 100 percent effort, but I got paid five hundred dollars and she got paid two thousand dollars, isn't that an unmistakable sign that luck was involved?

In my work and study of luck, I have discovered that it travels as freely as the wind and flows as easily as water. Luck is invisible, one of those irrational things that only blind faith can allow you to understand. If you want better luck, or if you want to benefit from luck, you must believe luck exists, as much as you can. Actually, it's all right even if you don't believe in luck itself. You can start by just being mindful of luck. Being aware of the idea of it will empower you to mobilize your willpower and examine everything in your life, from your attitude to your habits to your relationships, so you can make the necessary adjustments to improve your luck and welcome more of it into your life.

When the sun rises in Pyeongchang-dong and envelops my house with its radiant light, the trickling creek in my garden carries my gaze down the valley, flowing like the unstoppable passage of time. Every morning, a new day opens before my eyes, and I can see that my grandmother's words are coming true. I have indeed grown my fortune, and I'm not going to stop. I also want to continue learning how others manage to attract wealth and success.

THE REPLENISHING OF LIFE

In my mind, if there is an A, there has to be a B that follows. The result of 1 + 1 is 2, period. Realistic and rational, I've always had a head for numbers, even as a child. I could easily spot what people liked and what appealed to them. That hunch about people's tastes served me well when I was working in television or running a business. I aimed to touch people's hearts, which the shows and my products did.

The key to this success was the intuition that ran in my family. Thanks to that sharp sense, I was able to develop a talent that helped me create shows that appealed to a large audience. I became curious to know what people meant when they said someone was "good at sensing things" or "had a good hunch." Which do you think is more important: what's visible or what's invisible? Which do you feel has a bigger influence on the world? Which has the bigger influence on you? I think the most relevant question is: Which do you believe in more?

The talent of performers who sing and dance on stage, the perfect pitch of a pianist who captures the audience's attention, an actor's charisma that reaches you through the screen, the genius of a physicist who develops a theory that no one has thought of before—none of these things is visible. The excitement of the crowd or their fluctuating wave of emotions is also invisible, but you can feel it with your senses. I began to realize that a "hunch" or a "feeling" is not much different—

something invisible that can have great power. When I focused on keeping my senses wide awake, and I stayed connected to them, I could be successful at whatever I attempted. These early successes later enabled my thriving career as a TV producer. Every show I made was a hit. My achievements almost seemed superhuman, surprising everyone around me, including myself. It seemed I had an open road of endless success ahead of me. But all that joy and excitement were short-lived.

Soon my new projects started to fall apart suddenly, just when things should have been taking off. I became my own worst enemy and started making self-defeating decisions, motivated by impatience and a lack of perseverance.

The same happened later, at one of the other TV studios where I worked. At the time, broadcasting still had a bright future ahead. Because I was the youngest producer on the record, it was also highly likely I would get an even better job offer from another company. And yet, I worked there for exactly two years before I left, without an ounce of regret.

Somehow, I had found the time to start a new business. I set up a publishing house in my spare time and worked on books that became bestsellers. I secured a solid position in the publishing industry, generating revenue through innovative sales and aggressive marketing strategies that traditional publishers didn't use. The joy of success didn't last long this time either. I was restless, and I didn't know why.

I dipped my toe into another pool and came back to the world of television after I was approached by one of the most successful Korean broadcasting stations. I was recruited to a higher position than before and kept climbing the corporate ladder as I racked up success after success, implementing my ideas and bringing them to life. And yet I was powerless against a feeling inside that seemed to undermine me at every moment.

———•———

I had always considered myself a highly rational and reason-able person, but this time, even I had trouble understanding myself. Maybe I was losing my mind. Something was bothering me, even though I was hitting the jackpot with everything I did. I should have felt happy, but I wasn't.

Was I experiencing burnout? Was I unhappy with the monthly performance bonuses that I was getting? No, it wasn't that. Still, I felt like something was wrong, like I had gotten lost in the woods. The more popular my shows were, the stronger that sentiment grew. It didn't take long for it to become a certainty. One day when I was feeling particularly strange, I said to my supervisor:

"I'd like to turn in my resignation."

"But you've been doing so well! What's the matter?"

What was the problem? Why did I always have to throw away something that other people desperately wanted? I couldn't explain why I had to sabotage everything at a crucial moment when nothing was forcing me to do so. It wasn't just important decisions like quitting a job. There were too many other examples in other areas of my life for me to enumerate. I knocked everything over, no matter how big or small, just at the moment when a little more work would have yielded results that anyone would have envied.

When I announced my intention to leave my workplace, my colleagues' reactions were unanimous: They all tried to dissuade me. As I broke the news at home, my family had a meltdown. My parents discounted my unhappiness as a passing whim and advised me to simply stick it out. My professors and mentors also strongly disapproved of my sudden resignation.

Despite all that, I left. Because I had poured my heart and soul into my work, I had no regrets. I had left as if I was possessed, without thinking about my next steps. I couldn't hear anything anybody was telling me. My brain was screaming in protest even as my heart was convinced I had made the right decision.

As I considered what to do next, I remembered what my grandmother had told me, or rather, her words kept returning to me: "You will grow your fortune."

What did she mean? Maybe she had meant that I would grow not only my own fortune but also the larger idea of "fortune," whether it be mine or someone else's. Maybe that's what I was truly interested in.

Somehow, I had inherited my grandmother's gift for intuiting other people's fortunes. No logic allows me to explain how this inheritance has happened or even how it works. Still, I was sure of one thing: Mysterious coincidences and synchronicities, things that couldn't be explained, happened all the time in my life. I began to accept and become more curious about the "invisible world" my grandmother had described, and it unfolded before me as I started to work with my fortune and those of others.

My colleagues were upset by my departure. They were still living in a society where appearances mattered, and my leaving made them question their own work lives. I'd had the same questions about my own work life, but once I left that world, I felt serene. I thought: *The time has come for me to finally realize my potential!*

To be honest, I didn't feel any different. My daily life felt the same: I went to bed at my regular time. I woke up at the usual hour, except that I had begun to decipher the larger idea of "fortune" and money, and the daily grind no longer seemed to have any power over me. I discovered I was much happier than when I was hustling in my day job and trying to live up to, and surpass, other people's expectations. I could now see that the many misfortunes and obstacles I had encountered in my life were necessary precursors to the happiness I was beginning to feel. I started to understand the concept of "fortune" and make it into my life's work.

When I worked in the entertainment field, my job was to catch celebrities' images with a camera. Now, I catch people's fortunes. People come to me with a wide variety of questions and problems—the biggest, most serious one is the subject of money. Even if the phrase "money can't buy happiness" is repeated often, money is a symbol of how people understand their fortune and their luck.

It doesn't matter whether a person is rich or poor. Neither is immune to the anxiety that money induces. There are people whose only wish is to become rich. There are people who remain hopeful, even when they've lost everything.

People have so many questions about money: How can one be born rich? Is it possible to become wealthy if you weren't born with that luck? Many people tend to think that happiness is linked to money, which leads them to ask me all sorts of questions about it. Yes, they are asking me about money when they pose these questions, but in a way, they are also inquiring about their fortune and their luck. And about how they can attract more of these things in their lives.

—————

There is a time when everybody experiences a life change. In yeok-hak,[*] that moment is called gyo-woon-gi[†] or "transition period." As you can probably guess by the name, it's a period when a person's "current fortune" gives way to a "new fortune." When life leaves the past behind and moves forward, unforeseen changes occur. Oftentimes, people misunderstand the ensuing chaos as misfortune.

When someone asks a question like, "Sales keep dropping. Will my business survive?" I share my perspective from my experience of the world, which is completely different from theirs.

"Your fortune is currently going through a replenishing phase. You've reached a turning point in your life. Money also has phases. There is no need to worry. Just because you don't have any money now doesn't mean you never will. When you understand that the confusion of change is not misfortune, your situation will have changed."

I want to tell you the story of a curry restaurant in Osaka, Japan. At the beginning of the COVID pandemic, the owner

---

[*] Yeok-hak is the study of the *Book of Changes*, an ancient Chinese text on divination.
[†] Gyo (to cross) woon (luck) gi (period) is a point in time when the period dominated by one type of fortune ends and another begins. It's when your luck turns.

had to cut his business's hours for a long period, which left him with a considerable amount of rice that was going to go to waste. He was understandably distressed by the thought of throwing away so much rice—enough to feed several hundred people. As with many businesses during that time, everywhere he looked, it seemed there was misfortune, and his business would not be immune to it.

However, he quickly realized he needed to be creative, to find ways to adapt to this seeming misfortune. He started to look for other ways he could make use of the rice. He soon found a company in Singapore that manufactured beer from stale bread that was going to be thrown out. He contacted them and licensed their technology, which he then used to upcycle the rice. After a great deal of effort, he created his own craft beer made from his unused rice.

The media widely publicized the restaurant owner's inspiring story and his ingenious way of using rice that would have otherwise been discarded. In his attempt not to waste rice in a world suffering from food insecurity, a small curry shop owner turned into the founder of a craft beer business. What he had perceived as misfortune was, in fact, an auspicious transition to good fortune.

———•

A change in life patterns usually makes people anxious. They are terrified that the happiness and good fortune they are enjoying may suddenly disappear. However, I believe it is important to think about our individual fortunes in a different way. Imagine: There is not a single body of water on Earth that flows at the same speed at all times. Sometimes, the water will be agitated; at other times, it will be calm. Water ebbs and flows. A human life is no different. Those who know this are not perturbed when they experience a change in fortune. Some sense that during these times, they are actually well positioned to seek ways to attract better luck.

There is a term in Korean that essentially means "replenishing." It is a character so ancient and little used that you won't find it in a dictionary, but the word has long been used verbally in traditional Korean communities. Fishermen use the word when they describe an interesting natural phenomenon that is highly valued if you make your living from fishing. This "replenishing" describes the situation when a storm churns up the ocean's water and sands, causing it to become murky and making it a difficult time to catch fish. However, soon after the winds pass, the waters settle and become so clear that you would never guess there had just been a powerful storm. It is in the quiet after the storm, in the clear waters, when the big fish gather and are most easily caught.

I hope that this story of the fishermen and their concept of "replenishing" is a reminder that whatever hardship you are faced with, you should not easily despair or think your whole life has fallen into the abyss of misfortune. You may be going

through a replenishing phase—a storm of a different kind—
before your luck takes a turn for the better.

"ORDINARY" IS THE BEST COMPLIMENT IN THE WORLD

It was 2013. An ordinary young woman was preparing for an
exam. She was filled with self-confidence. Since she was a
young child, she had never known failure and had always believed in the power of diving into any challenge. She bravely
took the test but was eliminated in the first round. *It's okay. I
was unlucky*, she told herself.

The exam was known to be difficult, after all. It involved
both a written section and a personal interview with the examiners. She told herself she couldn't have expected to succeed on the first try. She started preparing for the exam a
second time. She dedicated all of her time to studying.

She applied for the exam a second time and felt confident.
She passed the first portion but didn't stay happy for long: She
learned that she failed the written portion. *This year is just not
my year*, she told herself.

She tried a third time the following year. But luck seemed
to evade her still. She blamed "that damn luck" for her failures.

After several failed attempts, she realized something important. During those years of test-taking, she had let the idea
of luck control her. Every time she failed, she would tell her-

self, *Luck is not on my side,* or *I had bad luck this time,* to feel better. She had been waiting for "the right moment" to bring her success instead of working toward her goal.

After two years, she gave up on the exam. The examiners were people, too. Their changing moods the day she took the oral part of her exam could easily sway the outcome, no matter how much she studied. She could adapt herself to immovable standards but not to imperfect, all-too-human circumstances. She was determined to make it by using her skills, instead of hoping to get lucky.

She decided she needed to find another way to show what she was capable of. She racked her brain trying to figure out how to do it. Eventually, she decided to find the answer outside the traditional avenues of open recruitment exams. Instead, she entered every talent or ability contest she could find: contests organized by the government, private companies, and even contests for public service announcement videos. Ultimately, she was awarded prizes in thirty-two different contests, and her story was featured in several news outlets.

Before long, a miracle happened. Her school contacted her on behalf of the company she had so wanted to join but whose exam she had failed multiple times. The company had heard about a miraculous student who had won every contest in the country, and it wanted to make her a special job offer, bypassing its traditional exam criteria. That is how, in 2016, that student joined SBS[*] as the youngest producer in the company's history.

Online, other students who were studying for the same exam to get an entry-level job at SBS enviously complimented her: "Wow, you're really lucky!"

It wasn't luck, however. I know, because I am that girl. What I did was work to improve my luck on my own. What if I had decided to waste another year, blaming bad luck for my successive failures? I could still be wasting my life away, convinced that I just had terrible luck.

Now, I can say with confidence that luck is real, but one should never rely entirely on luck for everything. Luck is something you work on, not something you count on. The moment you let luck take over, you lose power over your life.

That's the reason why you should strive to notice and gather any and all luck that crosses your path. From the lucky moments you notice every day (the bus that you caught just in time, the raffle for which you won second prize) to any truly extraordinary luck you experience (getting the big job you were not the leading candidate for, winning the lottery)—you

---

[*] SBS (Seoul Broadcasting System) is one of the leading South Korean television and radio broadcasters.

must try to make it all yours by working with it, not expecting it or assuming it will be yours forever.

LUCK IS A WATERWAY, AND FATE IS A BOAT

There was once a rich man who couldn't bear the idea of leaving behind all he had amassed after he died, so he prayed.

"Dear God, please let me take all of my wealth with me when I die."

The rich man's constant prayers reached God, who gave his permission.

"Exchange all your wealth for gold, and bring it with you."

The rich man died, but not before he had exchanged everything he had for gold. Finally, he arrived at heaven's door, carrying his heavy load of gold. Upon seeing him, the judge at the door asked the rich man:

"What did you bring all that gold for?"

"What do you mean?"

The rich man took a peek at heaven through the narrowly open doors. To his surprise, everything beyond the doors was made of gold, from the pillars to the floor, even including the walls. In heaven, gold was but an ordinary pebble.

"I had more money than I could spend in a lifetime, yet I had been carrying it with me all along, and for what?"

The rich man bitterly regretted his decision, but it was too late. He could no longer spend all, or even any, of his wealth.

People say the money you spend while you are alive is the

money that you truly own. If only the rich man had shared his wealth or spent it on himself and his loved ones during his lifetime, he would have left this world with a peaceful mind. Instead, he kept all of his money locked away without spending it, and in that way he was actually truly poor. He only appeared to be a rich man from the outside.

Luck is a waterway, and fate is a boat. Some people are born on a luxury yacht, and others are born on an ordinary ship. If you're unlucky, a raft is all you are given. Nevertheless, whether you are a rich person on a yacht or a poor person on a raft, everybody must navigate the waves on the boat they have. If your fate is defined by the type of boat you're on, how you ride those waves is entirely up to you, your abilities, and your will.

Of course, it matters what waterway you encounter. Its current can lead you toward a fortune that is either favorable or unfavorable. There would be no problem at all if it always flowed in the direction you wanted, but if you get caught on a wave that carries you in the opposite direction, you're in trouble. You must not stop rowing, lest your boat move in a direction you don't want to go.

That is how life is. Those born on a yacht can navigate with ease without worrying about strong waves. Those who are born on a regular boat or even a raft must constantly exert themselves to prevent the vessel from going in a direction they don't want to go or even capsizing.

The people on a yacht are those we think of as having been born with a silver spoon in their mouth. As soon as they arrive in this world, they already have riches and good prospects: company shares in their name, maybe they are already the designated heir to their family empire, future chaebols.[*] In Korea, we say, "Chaebols are God-given." The probability of being born as one is low. We must accept it as fate.

———•———

Would you like to be a rich person who has billions they will never spend? Or would you rather be a rich person with a more realistic amount of money who is not controlled by it?

People always express the desire to be rich in vague terms, without a concrete idea about the actual amount they want or need or what they would spend that money on if they had it. The reason may be because they have a thoroughly ordinary fate, not that of an heir to a chaebol.

Still, you mustn't lose hope. Although you aren't likely to become a billionaire, having an "ordinary" fate does not mean you can't be rich in a realistic way. Isn't having a reasonable

---

[*] Chaebols are large, industrial conglomerates in South Korea that exert huge power over its economy; can also be the family that controls them (e.g., Samsung). It is a combination of two words that mean "wealth" and "clan."

amount of wealth you can control and spend with a quiet mind much better than being rich in a showy way to impress others?

Most people are destined to have ordinary lives. Those who wish to be rich, however, grimace as soon as they hear the phrase *ordinary fate*. Deep down, everybody wants to be told they are destined for something special.

An ordinary physique, an ordinary job, an ordinary personality, an ordinary life. On the one hand, being "ordinary" or having an "ordinary fate" means nothing separates you from the crowd; on the other hand, it means nothing makes you a lesser being either. This interesting distinction is lost on many people. If you think about it, "ordinary" is the best compliment in the world.

I use the allegory of an archery target to explain this concept to the people who don't like the word *ordinary*. Let's say there is a target called "life" fifty feet ahead of you. The score ranges from ten points to zero from the bull's-eye outward. Theoretically, your first arrow would hit eight, which is the average. Your second arrow flies off target due to the wind. The world of luck works differently. Regardless of whether there is a storm or an earthquake, no arrow ever goes outside the target. With enough focus, it is even possible to hit the bull's-eye in adverse conditions. That's because "ordinary" implies that, even if your shot is not outstanding, in life, your arrow never fully misses the target.

As you can see, the word *ordinary* has a complexity that

you might not suspect. Being ordinary—always getting an eight—is actually difficult to achieve. If you look at it from a different viewpoint, it means that you are always somewhere inside the range of luck, never outside the game completely. Another way to see this is to understand that you can always build your fate by yourself. If you practice archery, you will get better at it. Life can be the same way.

In an ordinary life, it is more likely that you will be a person who doesn't just keep their fortune locked up somewhere but actually spends it. If you haven't been lucky enough to be born one of the 1 percent, you can aim to be one of the 99 percent of wealthy people who hold their money in their hand and spend it where, when, and on what they want and need.

That is what it truly means to have an "ordinary fate."

THE WRONG QUESTIONS TO ASK ABOUT MONEY

As word of my ability to read people's fortunes spread, many came to me for a consultation: a member of one of the top chaebol families in the country, a politician who had an upcoming election, and celebrities trying to choose their next projects. Ordinary office workers, too. Even though everyone had their own story and their own concerns, the most frequently asked questions were always about luck that attracts money: "Am I going to become rich?"

Some people have questions about how to live a better life

and how to be more successful: "When will it be my turn to be lucky?"

Everyone is curious about their future. I was no different. I used to read the monthly horoscope section in magazines with great interest. I would get excited by a tarot reading as if it were going to transform my entire life. Even that faint glimmer of hope made my heart pound. It made me feel like I could seize the future in my hands, however elusive that future might actually be.

The truth is that the principle of luck is not straightforward in the same way that money is strictly transactional. Luck is not an automated system that can suddenly bring you a brand-new life, like a karaoke machine that plays new songs as long as you supply it with coins.

One day, I went to see my doctor because of a severe headache.

"What brings you in?"

"I have a splitting headache."

"Let's do a checkup first. I need to figure out what's causing your headache."

A doctor's first job is to diagnose. A good doctor identifies the cause of your illness and then afterward, they present different ways to heal the illness, be it surgery, a pharmaceutical prescription, or even just rest. The patient can then choose the program that suits them best based on the doctor's diagnosis.

Ultimately, it is always the patient who must make the final decision about which option to subscribe to.

I've discovered in my work that deciphering each person's luck is not much different. Some people worry about money or marriage. Others worry about moving jobs or their businesses. They all expect me to give them the exact answer to their questions, but very few get what they want. I answer them truthfully, but they are not prepared to fully accept my answers.

———•———

A client told me he had been working as an assistant manager at a small distribution company for the last three years. He came to me, expecting that I would dispense a special prescription that would turn him into a rich man overnight.

As soon as he sat down, he asked me with a smile: "Everyone has always told me I had great saju. But nothing special happened in my twenties. Now I have reached my thirties, but I feel like things are still not working out for me. At this point, I should have at least won the lottery or something, don't you think?"

He seemed so confident. He gave me a look that seemed to tell me that life must have incredible luck in store for him, but somehow it had gotten lost on its way. It was as if it were my responsibility to get it back on track.

"May I ask you what it is precisely that you want?"

"I must become rich. Am I going to be rich? Will my life improve in the next three years?"

He then went into great detail about the success and money-filled days he was sure would unfold in the next three years. It made me ask him: "What were you doing three years ago?"

"I was working at the company I'm at now. Getting a regular paycheck for hardly any work doesn't feel so bad."

He had revealed his future self to me. His life three years ago was precisely what his life would be three years from now.

His fortune looked quite simple to me: If you do nothing, nothing will happen. This is the most natural truth in the world. At thirty years of age, was he really unaware of such a basic fact? He was completely ignoring a fundamental rule of luck, or rather, of life. I had no advice to give someone who wasn't doing anything but hoping for a windfall.

Meanwhile, he kept staring at me, his desperate eyes screaming: "Please tell me I'll become rich. I beg you."

Like a doctor, I assess the situation and make a diagnosis. I never give any answers. What I do is put my head together with my client's and we strive to find ways to change their life for the better. I take seriously anyone who is determined to change their lives; then I give them all the advice they need. However, there is nothing I can say to someone who comes to see me and just expects me to tell them exactly what they want to hear.

I wanted to speak candidly to my client, at least about luck, so this is what I told him: "Desperation drives luck away. You cannot rely on the luck you're given. You must make your own. There are several ways to grab luck. You must find them."

Even bumblebees need a reason to fly toward something. Even a wildflower on the side of the road must spread its scent and pollen, a survival strategy for its fragile being that nature has helped put in motion but that the flower must do itself. The rules are the same when it comes to luck. To be lucky means nothing more than being given good timing and a favorable set of circumstances for good things to come into being. But in the end, you are the one who must put in the work to make sure your luck becomes tangible and real in your life.

The young man had asked me the wrong question to begin with. Rather than "Am I destined to become a rich man?" he should have asked me, "How can I turn luck in my favor?" Even better would have been for him to ask himself that question before coming to me.

As the man turned to leave, I could see he was disappointed. I watched his back recede from me and could see his luck drifting even further away.

Changes and Signs That Signal a New Long-Term Fortune

It is said that a person's long-term fortune changes every ten years. It also should be noted that change occurs at different times for every person. The one- to two-year period preceding a new long-term fortune is called gyo-woon-gi. During gyo-woon-gi, each person experiences the same types of events, without exception. They may be something good; they may be something bad. But what is certain is that during this period, the incoming fortune crosses paths with the outgoing fortune, causing unprecedented confusion and conflict.

A new long-term fortune never comes unannounced. We are warned of its arrival through changes in our bodies, minds, and environments. Telltale signs of this incoming change in fortune can be physical, like an alteration in our complexion, or spiritual, as you find yourself drawn to new values. Or your environment might change as you find yourself surrounded by different people and your relationships evolve with them in new ways. Such changes and signs allow us to not only gain insight into our present fate, but to also begin to get a sense of our near future.

While luck is said to change every ten years and thus flows in and out a number of times in an average lifespan, it is said that people will only experience a tide of great good fortune during one or two of these transition periods. In other words, it's a phase that everybody goes through a few times in their lives. The successes, failures, abundance, or impoverishment of one's life depends on how acutely you perceive these signs of change, so that you can lean in and work with your luck to take advantage of them. You must do everything in your power not to miss a new long-term change in fortune when it is about to arrive.

Below are a number of common changes and signs that occur at a gyo-woon-gi. Do you sense a change coming?

* Your facial expression brightens.

* Your tastes or affinities change.

* The people who make up your social circle change.

* Changes occur in your environment because you move jobs or houses or get married.

* You suddenly have a better appetite.

* Your houseplants blossom and grow healthily.

* You go through a troubled phase as you are hit with misfortune.

* You become a part of new groups and social communities.

- It feels easier to get up in the morning.

- Your perspectives and attitudes change.

Can you look back on your life and see other periods when similar signs and changes heralded the arrival of a long-term change in fortune?

The Psychology of
WILL

2

To Conquer or Be Conquered by Luck

THE WIND THAT PUSHES THE SAILBOAT

"My mother is very ill. Is she going to be all right?" asked the young woman who had come to see me about her mother's health.

"Is it serious? Has she seen a doctor?" I asked.

"She's done all kinds of exams. They haven't found anything, but she's awfully weak and keeps collapsing," she replied.

The young woman was deeply concerned. The youngest of her siblings, she looked no older than thirty and still had something youthful about her. I could tell she must have been worried about her mother for a long time, for her sunken eyes bore evident signs of fatigue.

I empathized deeply with her, perhaps because we were about the same age. Her heartfelt devotion was almost palpable. I quickly recomposed myself, hoping I would be able to relieve her worry even a little bit, but I was perplexed. My intuition was telling me that her mother was in far greater danger than it seemed. I was hesitant. Was it wise to be so brutally honest to a worrying daughter? In any case, I couldn't ignore her mother's situation when she appeared to be in such a vulnerable state. I made a suggestion, hoping her condition would improve at least a little.

"Stay close to your mother, even if there seems to be no major problem. It's important."

"I will."

———•———

A few months later on a hazy morning, I received a call around eleven o'clock. It was the young woman who had desperately sought help for her mother. With a trembling voice, she informed me of her mother's passing.

"There was nothing we could do," she said.

Had I failed to detect a sign from fate? That thought suddenly filled me with regret. I assumed she had been involved in a freak accident. I could not have been more mistaken.

The cause of death was suicide. She had been suffering from depression. Who could have ever predicted that a seventy-four-year-old woman would take her own life? As people advance into old age, they usually focus on staying healthy to live longer. It was difficult to imagine that a woman of her age would commit suicide. Even with the strong intuition I had had about her life, I had not foreseen that the mother's will-power would come into play.

Willpower is such a potent force! I thought to myself.

The experience of sensing the mother's struggles but not foreseeing how she would respond to them taught me something: Willpower plays such a critical role in a person's fate that it can make the difference between life and death.

From time to time, I meet people who look like they're going to take their own lives, however vague that impression may be. Practitioners of the science of Myeongli[*] say that you can read such things by using a person's birthday to interpret their saju. I don't work with Myeongli and birth times. In my case, I had envisioned the mother wrapped in thick clouds, but it didn't feel like a sign, or at least I could not understand it as one, that she would commit suicide.

Human willpower is particularly effective when it comes to money. I have stressed this point before, but "luck with money" is little more than being given a favorable set of circumstances to help one acquire wealth. Think of it as the wind pushing a sailboat. What you choose to do with that

---

[*] The study of saju.

wind and where you channel your energy depend on you. I have seen a lot of people challenge their destiny and achieve success on their own. It's easy to find examples; some are famous worldwide. Becoming rich is within your power by the use of your will, and it becomes easier to accomplish if you understand how to work with any wind of luck that pushes your boat.

Son Jeong-eui, the CEO of SoftBank, is said to be the richest man in Japan. A third-generation Zainichi Korean,[*] he grew up in an illegal shack and was so poor he even contemplated dying. But the starving young boy has become the wealthiest man in Japan today. Who would have predicted he could achieve such great success, coming from absolutely nothing?

The same goes for the CEO of the Adani Group. Chairman Gautam Adani is a self-made man who was listed as the third richest person in the world by Asiana Times. He is a force of nature who became a first-generation self-made man in India. India is a hierarchical society rigorously ruled by a caste system. The rule is that rich people are born into wealthy families. And that's the reason why most business tycoons in India come from wealth, running the family business that was

---

[*] Zainichi (literally "residing in Japan") Koreans are ethnic Koreans living in Japan. Many Koreans moved to Japan during and after the occupation period. While the Japanese empire sought to assimilate them, the postwar Japanese government stripped ethnic Koreans of their citizenship and their rights. To this day, the Zainichi largely remain stateless, vulnerable to social and economic exclusion.

passed down to them. Not Chairman Adani. Born into an ordinary middle-class household, he started a small trading company that grew steadily until he became the third wealthiest man in the world. His success was unusual, even on a global scale, as it made headlines around the world.

Both Chairman Son, who had a difficult childhood, and Chairman Adani, with his unremarkable background, were nobodies in the past. The fact that these two men became big names in the world economy without anyone's help is truly inspiring. Furthermore, their examples prove the importance of willpower in building one's way toward wealth.

Chairman Son once said in an interview: "Everybody encounters luck at least once, but very few make something of it."

———

Instead of the outdated wisdom that said success is 70 percent luck and 30 percent effort, today I hear people say it is 90 percent luck and 10 percent effort. This new phrase underlines how difficult people feel it is to achieve anything without luck, but I don't entirely agree with that assessment. The best luck in the world means nothing without will. I'll go so far as to say that miracles of success and fortune never happen to people who have little willpower.

Between a kind person and a strong person, who do you think will have an easier time becoming wealthy? Naturally, the answer is the latter. Of course, a strong person who is also kindhearted could become even wealthier, but a rich person's luck only comes to those who have the capacity to accept it and work with it when they get lucky. Rich people have a much stronger will than you might think. At every moment, they are vigilant so they can seize good luck when it crosses their paths.

WHY DO THE WEALTHY FIXATE ON LUCK?

One of the most common tropes in soap operas is rags to riches, when the main character's life is transformed after they turn out to be the offspring of an affluent family. You could say that the triumph of good over evil is the principal message in stories like Cinderella or Kong Jwi and Pat Jwi.* Similarly, rags to riches is a subplot that has never failed to capture the public's interest. I think it's safe to say that nearly every one of us has dreamed of a better life and lived that dream vicariously by watching TV shows.

Now, let's imagine you have suddenly become the recipient of a massive inheritance. How would you feel upon learning that a distant relative you've never met has left you billions? On TV shows, the protagonist's first reaction—apart from surprise—

* Cinderella is French; Kong Jwi is Korean.

is to undergo a complete makeover, as if to make up for everything they had missed during their poor Cinderella stage.

You follow them around as they go on a shopping spree, gracefully hopping from one luxury boutique to another. They spend thousands of dollars on a Hermès Birkin bag made of Himalayan crocodile skin from the Himalayas, pay several more thousands for Dior shoes, and buy entire jewelry sets from high-end brands with their assistant at their heels, both hands full of shopping bags. A few items can quickly amount to fifty thousand dollars, and that's all they seem to do during the entire episode.

Watching such unrealistic scenes can feel all too real, even if what's happening is purely fictional. You wonder whether the main character is going to have any money left, no matter how rich they are.

Imagine you have suddenly come to possess a ten-million-dollar fortune and start spending fifty thousand dollars every day. With expenses that total one and a half million dollars a month, that sudden windfall of family assets will never last. At that rate of spending, you'd have less than a year before you find yourself completely destitute again.

They never show you bank balances in those dramas. It is left to the viewers to guess what happens to the main character in ten years.

Although it is not impossible to become a billionaire

overnight, how you work with the money you get is a different story. No matter how much money fortune brings you, it will all be pointless if you are not equipped to receive it. And in that case, you could get caught in a whirlwind beyond your control, embroiled in difficult, draining situations. I learned this through the stories of two wealthy families that I've met in real life.

The first family had a colossal fortune, thanks to the land the family had acquired during the Japanese occupation. The father's assets had grown in value to well over fifty million dollars. He and his wife had one concern: Their two sons, in their thirties, were still incredibly immature.

As he reached his seventies, the father started reflecting on how to manage his land and property, his inheritance. He wondered how best to pass it down so his sons would keep it safe. He did not even expect them to increase the family's wealth. His only wish was that they would at least preserve what he himself had inherited from his ancestors over the generations. Contrary to their parents' wishes, however, the two brothers kept proposing nonsensical business ideas.

"We have a nice view from here. Let's build a hotel."

"A food and beverage business is the way to go, Dad. We should open a big café."

The elderly couple grew more troubled by the day. They couldn't understand why their sons were deluding themselves with pipe dreams instead of taking care of the family assets. Tensions rose between the sons, who were asking their parents to invest in their business ideas, with no oversight. The elderly couple determined that their sons' business ideas were unrealistic and not likely to succeed. Eventually, the conflict became too distressing for their aged father, who started spending an increasing amount of time in his sickbed. He and his wife drifted apart from their children, who ultimately moved out of the house as the tension became difficult to bear.

In a meeting I had with them, the elderly couple told me: "The only thing we want from our sons is that they preserve our heritage. We don't even expect them to increase it. If they could just keep it safe and avoid getting scammed . . ."

The sons, however, thought differently. In their meeting with me, they said: "We could make so much money, but our parents are too old-fashioned. How can you expect to gain anything from all that land if you just hold on to it and do nothing?"

But it was already too late. The couple's health had deteriorated from a long, drawn-out illness that was compounded by all the other difficulties of old age. Their worries had led to discord, and eventually their money brought about another unfortunate event: The old couple passed away, alone on their deathbeds, neither of their sons by their side.

The parents feared losing luck, while the children coveted it but without a good idea for how to receive it. After they finally got their inheritance, the two sons soon squandered 80 percent of it on senseless business plans.

———

Let me tell you the story of another rich man. He started a small gaming company, which he grew into a global corporation within ten years. He was undeniably a capable individual. When he was growing up, his family had been so poor they hadn't even been able to afford his tuition fees. Still, the entrepreneur from a disadvantaged background rose to the top in a field dominated by the highly educated.

Of course, it was no easy feat. He started his first company with one hundred thousand dollars, which he raised by borrowing money from his friends and family. The business failed not too long after. However, he was determined to succeed.

"My beginnings may be humble, but my future will be glorious."

He picked himself up and started a second business. The result? He turned it into a medium-sized company that employs about one thousand people and records more than one billion dollars in annual revenue.

The way he raised his children was equally remarkable. Following his beliefs, he had them earn their own money, raising them to be autonomous individuals who didn't depend on their parents. Moreover, he declared he would not hand over his business to his children. He would hire a professional who would ensure his company was managed transparently, even after his departure.

He also decided to give back to society, generously and without hesitation. Although his children may have felt hurt by their father's decision at first, they quickly set out to work on their own dreams. They followed in the footsteps of their parents, who always acted according to their beliefs and matched their words with their actions. People praised the family's accomplishments in unison.

"He did such a good job with his children."

"That's not all, look at his company!"

The eldest child founded a small start-up, taking after his father, while the youngest began building a career in the arts.

The wealthy man in this story has nothing left to worry about. He is just waiting for the day he will be able to enjoy old age in peace and calm.

This is how different two individuals can be, despite both being rich. The former is preoccupied with clinging to the wealth he was born into. The latter has a more proactive attitude in expanding his money because he's built his own destiny as a wealthy man.

Of the two, who do you think is more concerned about

luck? Most people think it's the latter. In fact, both of them cared a lot about luck. They just approached it differently. The former was easily affected by luck, whereas the latter did not let it perturb him. If I had to choose between the two, I would say the rich man in the first story was the one more preoccupied with luck.

The old couple were conscious of their luck. They were well aware of the fact that they didn't owe their fortune to any effort of their own. That thought made them live with a life-long fear that they might lose the luck they had been granted.

Of course, some may think it's silly to worry about something like that. However, the fundamental knowledge that they received their money with no effort on their part had instilled in them the idea that money is a source of anxiety, almost as a natural consequence, which is ironic because they were so aware that they'd had no control over how they got so lucky to begin with. In their minds, their luck could leave them as easily and quickly as it had come. This explains why those who are born rich can't help but be highly sensitive to luck.

By contrast, wealthy people who are dedicated to their day-to-day lives have such a laid-back attitude toward luck that it's almost hard to believe. It doesn't mean they don't believe in it. Only that they put more faith in their abilities than in luck, because they have paved the way to their destiny. The thought that their life might fall apart is not a significant source of anxiety. They are the ones who built that life in the first place.

That is probably the reason why they get back on their feet like a Weeble Wobble toy even if they lose everything. Bad luck doesn't trouble them. What led them to success is their willpower, which remains unwavering regardless of the fluctuations of luck.

The wealthy "up there"—the rich from birth—are easily affected by luck. The wealthy "down here"—those who win—focus on luck. In other words, the former get crushed under the weight of luck, letting it wash over them, whereas the latter use it as a stepping stone for growth. That is the secret of the wealthy who are equipped to bear the burden that comes with money.

BREAKING THE CYCLE OF DESPAIR

How big of a role can willpower play in shaping your life? Is willpower enough to attain success and wealth? These questions are half right and half wrong.

Willpower expresses one's desire for a particular outcome. It must be followed by an action to make that outcome a reality. Always thinking and never acting is like counting Bitcoins in your head when you haven't got a penny to your name.

An acquaintance of mine was preparing for the bar exam.

Having freshly graduated from law school, he was getting ready for the first bar exam of his life. To him, however, it was also the last. His family was in a difficult situation. The love and sacrifice of his single mother allowed him to graduate from a reputable university in the Seoul area.[*] Still, he felt a lot of pressure about having stayed in school so long instead of starting to earn a living immediately out of high school. He was torn between his responsibility as head of the household and his desire to become a successful lawyer.

He couldn't stop ruminating over those thoughts while he was studying and attempted to appease his anxious mind by loitering in internet cafés. When he couldn't bear it anymore, he consulted a fortune-teller about the exam.

"I'm about to take a very important exam. Will I be successful?"

The fortune-teller, who was studying his birth date, interjected:

"What exam? There is no gwan[†] in your saju."

"What do you mean?"

"What I mean is that exams aren't going to take you anywhere."

He couldn't believe what he had just heard. Fail. He went

---

[*] Koreans tend to consider any university located in Seoul to be better than one in a province.

[†] In saju, *gwan* means "public office," the type of job the exam he was taking leads to, if he passed it.

to another fortune-teller, but they also told him he would fail. He visited ten of them, only to obtain the same result.

Exactly one year passed. That friend was admitted to the bar as the new year began. How could that be? When I heard what had happened, I couldn't help but nod in relief for him. As he had been preparing for the bar exam the first time, he had been walking right into failure, and not just because the fortune-tellers said so.

Too distracted by the pressure from his family to focus, he had been wasting time playing games. He had barely been attending class and had started drinking too much. He had given up and stopped making any effort. It would not have been a surprise if he did not pass the bar. Fortunately, being told he would fail by the fortune-tellers shocked him into sanity. He pulled himself together, eager to prove everyone wrong.

"Me? Fail? Fate can't beat me."

From that moment, he dedicated every waking hour to his studies. He had to. He was indebted to his mother and had to start looking after his family. His ceaseless efforts brought him closer to success. He used his willpower to get back on the right trajectory. Finally, he beat the odds and landed a job at the most renowned law firm in Korea.

His story clearly showed me that, with enough willpower, it is possible to reverse the course of fortune. Even if you are riding waves in the opposite direction of the wind, you can turn your boat around if you row twice or three times as hard. If you are going through an unlucky phase, then grab your oar even tighter and fight like hell to stay afloat.

———•

The film *Eat, Pray, Love* starring Julia Roberts features the famous story of a man who came to pray on his knees every week in front of a statue of Saint Mary.

"Please, let me win the lottery."

The man prayed fervently every day, his eyes filled with tears. He was always there, no matter what, hands joined in prayer. Exasperated, Mary finally spoke to him. She said: "I'll grant you your wish, but please, at least buy a ticket."

If your dream is to win the lottery and live a new life, the least you can do is to look for the famous lottery shops or analyze the power of numbers and identify those that will increase your chances of winning. At the end of the day, the winner is someone who got up and went to a store to buy a lottery ticket. Money is no different. If you don't have any money right now, you must first decide how much money you want to have and how you're going to get it.

I'll give you an example. Let's say you want a luxury car that costs one hundred thousand dollars. You expect your income to increase slightly during the next two years, so that's the time you give yourself to buy the car. This means you have to save at least fifty thousand dollars a year, in other words, four thousand dollars a month, one thousand dollars a week, or one hundred fifty dollars every day. Then you must stop to think whether it's even possible to save that much money with an ordinary job.

After some basic calculations, you realize that two years is too short to save that amount given your income. So you start making more realistic plans, like saving two thousand dollars every month for five years. That is what you call a plan B, with a different objective or a longer timeline. That is how you buy a luxury car. Albeit rare, people who achieve their goals do exist.

Sometimes, it can feel like you're pouring in 100 percent of yourself and only getting a 50-percent return, while someone else gets a 200-percent return for putting in the same amount of effort. That's a sign that luck is at play. Either way, you can't expect luck to simply fall into your lap while you are sitting on your hands; you must put in the effort at all times, so luck can supercharge your efforts when it does arrive.

Insatiable greediness is a harmful trait, but so is hopeless apathy. Successful people all do what it takes, then seize the luck when it arrives and try to make it when it doesn't. In the end, money is an external factor, just like work or people. To make it yours, you need to work for it. Only when you are competent and mature enough not to be swayed by the comforting idea that luck will solve everything, can you live with the mindset of a wealthy person, confident that you have the wisdom to have command over your fortune and how to grow it.

WHAT "I WAS LUCKY" REALLY MEANS

"I was lucky."

That's what Son Heung-Min, the first Asian player to win the Golden Boot in the English Premier League, said in an interview. Singer Park Jin-Young[*] would also frequently tell his interviewers he attributed 30 percent of his success to hard work and 70 percent to luck. Could it be they are humble-bragging? I don't think so; both Son and Park ascribe too much of their achievements to luck for that to be true. Both reached the top of their field. They don't need any more fame, and in terms of skill and influence, they are well established in their current positions. Then why do they keep saying that so much of their success is due to luck?

I've always been particularly curious when it comes to the luck of people who reached the top of their fields. They must have failed multiple times before they achieved success. In their cases, I mean failure in the sense of a small, unpredictable factor that completely overturned what they had expected despite their preparation and effort.

For a soccer player, an example might be a strong wind in

---

[*] The founder of JYP Entertainment, most well known for producing artists such as g.o.d., Miss A, TWICE, and Stray Kids, among others.

the stadium that messes up a perfect goal kick or having tangled shoelaces. For a singer, it might be a sore throat the day before a contest, upsetting their hopes for a top spot in the final ranking. In ascribing so much of their success to luck, Son Heung-Min and Park Jin-Young were granting more importance to fleeting moments than to their effort. In other words, they were ready because they had done everything that was in their power to do, but they also understood and accepted that there were moments of good (and bad) luck outside of their control.

———•

I recently came across an interesting article about people who had left their jobs after less than two years. They were asked what had made them quit. As you might expect, the majority of the reasons were related to the conditions in their workplace. The number one cause was "a strained relationship with one's boss or coworkers," followed by "incompatibility with the organizational culture," "subpar welfare benefits," "responsibilities that didn't fit one's aptitudes," and "the company's lack of vision." One answer in particular drew my attention: "Lack of opportunities offered for development and advancement."

Businesses operate on employees' labor. Did it make sense to say the businesses weren't giving their workers opportunities that would help both the employee and the company?

I remembered when I had just begun my television producer job. It was the job of my dreams, and I was walking on air thinking about all the programs I would create. I had already proven I was capable by winning contests. I felt I had a deep understanding of popular trends and was ready to create audience-winning shows. All I had left to do was to start creating.

I was twenty-seven at the time, and the youngest producer at the station. Before me stood a whole cohort of senior producers. Far from producing shows, I was immediately relegated to assistant producer. As I completed the odd jobs assigned to me, I thought: *I can be as good as them. Why won't anybody give me a chance?*

As the days went by, I became more and more disgruntled. I was exhausted and frustrated. One day, I finally made up my mind.

That's it. I'm not going to wait until somebody hands me an opportunity.

I worked all night for an entire week and used the little downtime I had during the weekend to work on my own project: a literal self-made show. I made a parody in a music video format and uploaded it to the internet. The response was overwhelming.

The timing was favorable. When the video hit one million views, another broadcasting company asked to use my clip. I saw no reason to refuse. By word of mouth, my homemade video spread wider and wider through the internet. A few days later, I got called into my boss's office.

"Have you lost your mind? How dare you send your work to a competitor?"

I got a severe reprimand, but I had something to say for myself. I candidly explained that all I wanted was to do broadcasting work, so I had found a way to make it happen. I think he was both annoyed and impressed. And just like that, I got to produce a show of my own.

———•———

When things don't work out as expected, people tend to look for an explanation outside themselves. They either blame others or their environment, just like the people in the survey who said they weren't being given any opportunities at work.

Of course, it is possible that your workplace is stifling your talent and denying you chances to realize your potential. But from a different perspective, it also means that you are responsible for not demonstrating your competence. If you're only given level-three tasks when your actual skill level is ten, that's because level three is exactly where you appear to be. Life doesn't gallantly roll out the red carpet and go, "It's your turn. Show us what you've got!" If you are genuinely competent, you should be able to show it to others, whether your current context allows it or not. You can't call yourself truly skilled until you can confidently display your abilities to the world.

Money is the same as skills. No matter how intense your desire for money is, it's certainly not enough to just get hold of it; just as it is not enough to have skills if you don't find a way to display them. It takes effort and energy to make something yours. In the end, the key to attracting money is the ability to create opportunities for it.

Luck is the sweet reward bestowed upon those who carry things through, regardless of the circumstances. Has the phrase "I was lucky" become clearer now? Not only must the basic, crucial requirements (hard work and skills) be met, but the weather needs to be nice as well. Nearly all the wealthy people I've met have said the same thing. If you are currently an ordinary salaried worker who has resolved to become rich one day, you need to think through the true meaning of the phrase "I was lucky," and come up with opportunities to demonstrate your abilities.

THE PARADOX OF WORK-LIFE BALANCE

There was a beautiful actor who appeared on a television show in Korea. Her radiant beauty made heads turn, and her slender physique was reminiscent of a willow branch.

The word *beauty* followed her around like a nickname before she even debuted on TV. People in the neighborhood praised her, saying she could be Miss Korea. She would get stopped on the street by casting agents while on her way to meet a friend. Street casting was actually how she first got into the entertainment industry. She was aware she was good-looking. She was ready to be discovered and blossom, and the cameras were ready for her.

Her ultimate goal was to become rich, and it looked like she would succeed if she put her mind to it. Exclusive modeling fees, advertising fees, and opportunities to become a brand ambassador, adding up to several hundred thousand dollars, awaited her. She was counting the days until those dreams of wealth would turn into reality.

Her acting career had begun smoothly. She was able to land a supporting role relatively quickly thanks to her agency's unreserved support and her outstanding looks. Her acting skills were still wanting, but viewers welcomed the appearance of a young new talent. All that was left for her was to climb her way to stardom. As her popularity grew, she started a jewelry business with a close friend. She wanted to show off her fashion sense and make additional money.

It soon became clear that she could barely withstand any hardship, maybe because she was used to receiving attention and being loved unconditionally since early childhood. It didn't take long for her to lose interest in anything that she started, and she gave up rather quickly. Because she hadn't endured many hardships, she lacked perseverance and patience.

This, in turn, made it difficult for her to stick with anything, and she repeatedly gave up before she made any significant achievements in her endeavors.

Two years after her debut, she was filming a new series under the hot lights of the soundstage. She came to see me, moaning.

"Min Ji, I'm having such a hard time."

"What? Why?"

"I liked playing the youngest daughter in that other drama; it was easy. This time, I have so many lines, and I feel too warm in my hanbok.* We always film deep in the mountains in the middle of nowhere, and I'm constantly made to do action scenes when I obviously have no coordination. Plus, I haven't been able to sleep properly in days, so on top of everything, my skin is a disaster."

"Hang in there, it's going to be over soon."

"But work-life balance is important to me."

I couldn't believe my ears. Those three words, *work-life balance*, seemed so mismatched with her desire to have a long-lasting, lucrative career. Was she expecting to have a balanced

---

* Hanbok, literally "Korean clothing," is the traditional Korean costume. Nowadays, hanbok are more typically worn during formal occasions, such as weddings.

life working in the cutthroat world of entertainment, where countless hardworking stars were constantly rising and falling? This was not a regular job in a predictable industry. Although I didn't show it, I was taken aback. I thought back to my own time trying to make my career in the entertainment business behind the scenes. While I would have loved to have a better work-life balance, it just wasn't the nature of the industry. Long hours, top-notch skills, and dedication were expected of everyone in front of and behind the camera.

I laughed it off at the time and commiserated gently with her. I treated it like the silly complaint of an endearing younger sibling. After all, she was an actor who was just starting her career, endowed with all the physical attributes required for the job and to be worshipped by all. I didn't imagine she would always avoid any challenge; I assumed she would eventually get used to the stresses and strains of the industry and have a successful career. That was the case for many actors, singers, and other celebrities I had met.

When I think of her story now, I regret that I did not give her more feedback and tough love. If I could go back in time, I would be more straightforward with her. I would tell her everything I could decipher about her fortune.

I would tell her that you can't expect to achieve something long-lasting and important to you if you shy away from difficulty and discomfort at every turn. While preserving a healthy work-life balance is a worthwhile goal, you still need to use every opportunity to demonstrate your skills and grit, especially if your dream is to become an actor with a "long-lasting, lucrative career." Just like the idea of winning the lottery, you can sometimes get lucky breaks, but you must lean in and work with them to make them last and become profitable.

I'd noticed that this was especially true in the world of the wealthy. There are likely a finite number of people who want to be a star, but there are as many people who want to be rich as there are grains of sand. Sometimes it seems as difficult to become rich as it is to pick a star from the sky. But many people who want to be rich seem to expect to achieve wealth without making a real effort. While there may be the odd exception, in truth, the world doesn't work like that.

"Work-life balance is important to me."

"I value personal freedom more than work."

People always say things like this, and it's not a matter of right or wrong. But it is about choice; "rich" in the monetary sense and "work-life balance" don't often mix well.

———•

If you want to work a moderate amount of time and make a moderate amount of money, that's fine. If you're comfortable with not becoming rich, it will be easier to create a life for yourself where you have a good work-life balance. But wanting to drive a Bentley when all you do is lie comfortably on your bed? Wanting to climb higher than others in your career while also living out every one of your desires, whether they be shopping, traveling, or resting? That's just unrealistic, not to mention impossible.

If you look at the world of entertainment, even the most sought-after top talents work day and night with few or no days off. Of course, some people face barriers even though they put in the time and give their very best. In my experience, those who stick with it always obtain good results, even if with a little delay. That's why I say to people who tell me their top priority is work-life balance to draw a clear picture of the kind of life they really want and to make choices based on that image.

Those who want to keep moving up may need to put aside their personal lives for periods of time. You can be the world's most competent, most successful CEO, but if you want to keep your business running well and growing, constant innovation and development are a must.

Managing a business is like riding a bicycle or a helicopter: You have to keep pedaling, and you have to make sure the rotor blades never stop spinning, lest you fall or crash. Constant stress is unavoidable, particularly if you have hundreds or thousands of employees dependent on you for their livelihoods.

CEOs are destined to live a life of self-control. That's why I consider the desire to be successful in business while maintaining a perfect work–life balance a contradiction. Those two things are mutually exclusive.

The young actor who wanted to become a top star but was not willing to commit to the sacrifices that would entail kept going from one easy role to the next, always playing a secondary role, often the daughter of an affluent family. Unfortunately, she was still being picky and only going to auditions if she liked the part.

One year passed, then two. Her appearances became fewer and farther between until she completely faded into obscurity. I wonder where she is now and whether she is still dreaming of a glamorous life.

HOW TO SUMMON YOUR WILLPOWER

Now you know how crucial willpower is in attracting good fortune. You also understand you must create your own opportunities and show others what you're capable of. But how do you summon your willpower to accomplish these things? How do you prepare yourself and put your plan into action? Some people foster a strong desire to become wealthy yet say they have no motivation. They claim they want nothing more than to make a lot of money, but at the same time, it all seems so unattainable to them; they don't know where or how to start. There is a very simple way to kindle willpower.

One day, a young entrepreneur came to see me, wondering if he should expand his business or not. From the moment he walked in the door, I noticed the glint in his eyes. He looked shrewd, and it was obvious he had a remarkably strong spirit. There was so much I could tell about him just by looking at his eyes. His pupils were radiating, as if to show the willpower and resolve that inhabited him. The entrepreneur spoke to me.

"I became exactly the kind of rich person I had envisioned, thanks to my restaurant business."

As I looked at his eyes, the image of several wealthy people flashed before my own. I thought to myself, *Oh, he's just like them.* New money with considerable wealth share a curious characteristic. They all have a distinct "rich-person image," without exception. It implies they have a precise idea of what kind of rich person they want to be and how rich they want to be.

"How did you become so successful?"

"I focused on one thing. I walked up the mountain every day to look at my house."

He was a renowned restaurateur who owned dozens of chain stores, from Italian restaurants to highbrow rooftop bars in Cheongdam-dong.* His business brought him no less

---

* The priciest district in Seoul, filled with upscale residences and designer boutiques. A US equivalent would be Beverly Hills or New York's Upper East Side. There is even a Rodeo Street in Apgujeong-dong, a neighboring district.

than one billion dollars in annual revenue. Today, he is a young and wealthy entrepreneur whose business is growing every year, thanks to the quality of his food and service. However, he hadn't gotten there easily; he had endured a lot of hardships in his childhood.

His father had worked in the meat wholesale business. Not a day went by without his father getting into some money trouble. Making ends meet was a constant struggle. The family barely survived on the wages his mother earned working at a restaurant. To make matters worse, one day his father lost all of the family's money, and they were evicted from their rental apartment.

The young entrepreneur barely finished school while living in a rented house in a slum. Until he moved to Seoul after graduating from high school, he lived in a home that flooded every time it rained. He was terrified of being made fun of at school because his uniform smelled like mold. And when he got back home, he had to worry about his house flooding again. To him, *home* was a word he wanted to reclaim, a lost childhood dream.

Ever since he'd gotten to Seoul, he'd kept one thing on his mind. He always repeated his dream: "I will buy my own house where I can live for the rest of my life!"

He then set out to realize his dream. He imagined a house in Gangnam, a neighborhood that has become symbolic of wealth, preferably with a view of the Han River. It would be perfectly protected from torrential rain and burglars. When he thought of "home," he could only think of one place. He didn't want to dream vaguely. So every night when he finished working, he headed straight to the nearby mountain.

From the top of the mountain, he could see his dream house on the other side of the Han River. Looking at the twinkling starlike lights of the home gave him the strength to push through another day as he imagined himself finally owning that house someday.

"X Apartment, Y-dong, Yongsan district, five billion won."

He repeated the characteristics of his future house like a spell. Determined to realize his dream, he had visualized everything about it, including the address and the shops around it.

He spent a few more years working at a restaurant, where he learned about all aspects of the food service industry. Penny by penny, he built up enough savings to fund his own business. After thoroughly calculating the profit and loss, he finally opened his first restaurant. It wasn't some dangerous, overambitious venture where he could end up buried in debt. He opened a small, well-planned restaurant with a simple concept that would be a slow and steady path, but one that was guaranteed to succeed.

He had thought about everything: the rent, the labor cost, the investment. Based on this perfect plan, he grew his business steadily for five years until he became a recognized, successful restaurateur.

When his restaurant turned a profit, the first thing he bought was his dream: the house he had thought about his whole life. With that purchase, he recovered his lost childhood. Who could have guessed that a young restaurant worker with no formal training whatsoever would become such a big player in the industry?

The young entrepreneur continued: "I think that's when I started focusing on a single goal. I wasn't even looking to amass a fortune. I just wanted enough money to buy a comfortable house so I could take care of my mother. Some people prioritize getting expensive foreign cars or luxury watches. For me, those things are secondary. People are so uncomplicated. What you value depends on the kind of life experience you've had. In my case, my objective was a house because that's what I lacked."

As I looked into his unwavering eyes, I knew without a doubt: *This person is going to become even richer.*

All successful people have something that sets them apart. The young entrepreneur was steadily concretizing the picture in his head. The "picture" I mention here is "what you're aspiring to achieve"—in other words, the "future" you want to realize.

The story of JTBC's* main anchor is another example that demonstrates its importance. That anchor was hired by the station after winning first place in a nationwide competition

---

* A highly popular South Korean cable TV network.

where the odds of winning were two thousand to one. When asked how he prepared himself for the exam, he answered: "I strengthened my heart every day by imagining working at the broadcasting station."

—•—

In a similar context, I think one can learn from the current trend of the "rich-person experience" by trying some of them. They will show you how much you really value the fruits of being a "rich person." As an example, you might try a multi-course meal worth several hundred dollars in a five-star hotel you wouldn't usually go to, or buy a first-class seat on a flight you can't afford with your current income. Some people may find fault with such reckless spending, but spending money like a rich person in order to understand what it would be like to become one can be a valuable experience.

When you've dined at a spacious table in an elegant dining room and had somebody take your coat and pull out a chair for you, when no effort is spared to make your experience pleasant from start to finish, you realize that kind of attention to detail is something you can't put a price on. If you come out of that experience convinced that the world a rich person lives in is sensational and you want to hold on to that feeling, you will find ways to turn your motivation into action and start building wealth.

But you needn't go to such expensive extremes to motivate

yourself. You can also start realizing your objectives by taking smaller steps along the way. In reality, we all live fragments of our lives in an affluent lifestyle, even if we're not always aware of it. For example, when you buy yourself nice clothes on credit at a department store for the first time in ages or reward yourself with a lavish dinner at the end of a particularly stressful day, you're treating yourself to a bit of luxury.

I'm not saying you should make YOLO your motto or live beyond your means. My point is that you should set concrete objectives for yourself and not hesitate to have a taste of the future you are building along the way. Don't content yourself with just stating you're going to make it big in the vaguest of terms. Your picture of a wealthy life should be so specific that it feels seared into your brain.

With a well-defined picture, your actions become more concrete, which increases your chances of hitting your target. A clear objective will make you less easily distracted, even if you lose perspective at times or your judgment becomes clouded. A person with a clear purpose is also more likely to maintain their drive and stay patient, making them less vulnerable to pointless worries. People whose dreams are so real that they are almost palpable always manage to grab them in the end. Specific thoughts lead to concrete results, while nebulous aspirations never become anything solid.

Picture yourself as a rich person and what you would like

to achieve as one. The more details you include, the stronger your desire for success will become. This is a simple yet effective way of reaching your goal.

There is a saying that goes, "Those who recognize good meat are the ones who have tasted it." You must achieve small victories before you can aim for bigger success. The young entrepreneur didn't need any advice from me. He already knew where he stood and what he needed to do. He may go through a couple of bad spells, like anybody. Even so, he knows he will never leave the ranks of the wealthy. I have no doubt he will keep achieving visible, concrete outcomes.

LUCK HAS AN EXPIRATION DATE

"Will I be happy in my old age?"

"Where will I be in ten years?"

People are always curious about the "end of life." They want to know whether they will achieve wealth in their later years and if they will have a comfortable life after retirement. In doing so, they fail to realize that life doesn't pan out according to some perfect scenario. There is no elaborate, predetermined itinerary, only a general direction. In the end, the detailed route is for you to design.

When I tell them this, people always ask, clearly disappointed: "Oh, but, is there no such thing as fate? Are you saying that saju and Myeongli are all lies?"

In the end, fortune consists of the past, the present, and the future combined. That's why nobody can predict the future. That's one of the essential lessons I learned from observing countless people.

Wealth is the same. Of course, a windfall is always possible. However, your chances of running into such luck are close to zero if you were born with the kind of ordinary fate where your arrows always land on the target but don't ever hit the center.

A common misunderstanding is believing that having good luck with money means you will come by a massive fortune later. Keep in mind that what you consider "being rich" and what money is worth to you are different for every person. Ten billion dollars might barely stir some people, while even a thousand dollars could release others from all sorts of torment.

It is worth thinking about: What does it mean to be lucky with money? And what price do we pay for money?

Simon led an ordinary, uneventful life. He worked as a part-time cashier at a supermarket. He would show up every day at the same time and mechanically scan barcodes during his shift.

One day, a customer told him: "You're going to have a lucky year with money next year."

The customer introduced themselves as a face reader.

Even if they were only saying it to be polite, it made Simon happy. In fact, from that day on, Simon started wearing a big smile on his face. Although he mostly thought *That will never happen*, a small, hopeful part of him had started whispering to himself, *Who knows?* and that voice grew ever louder.

So Simon waited in anticipation. He waited three months, which became six, then a year. A new year had begun, but still nothing. Simon was confused. He saw no signs of the windfall he was expecting. His hopeful expectation evaporated, leaving only disappointment.

In reality, Simon's good fortune had already passed him by. The previous year, Simon had been making two thousand dollars a month. The following year, his hourly wage had increased, which is very rare for a part-timer. The good fortune the face reader had seen in Simon's face had included that raise.

Good fortune with money doesn't mean you will become a billionaire overnight. All it means is that you will find yourself in a better, more abundant environment, where there will be more favorable conditions for you to make more money. In no way does it mean that a million dollars is going to fall from the sky into your hands, as Simon had imagined it would. When good monetary fortune is coming in your direction, in my experience, it is impossible to guess the amount. It could be one thousand dollars, or it could be one hundred thousand dollars.

Simon resented the face reader for not telling him the exact time and amount of his windfall. He did not realize that he was the one who had missed the opportunity. This is typical of people who have a misguided conception of how and when luck can arrive and don't have a good sense of what to do with it when it does.

If only Simon had thought, *Okay, I'm about to have good luck with money. Since I just got a raise, maybe I should use that money to invest in stocks, even if it's not much*, the story would have ended differently. If he had learned about investing and acquired some hands-on experience, he would have had a better sense of money, and because he was in a period of good financial fortune, the results may not have been bad at all.

If you want to win the lottery, you must at least buy a ticket. Good fortune with money is not an outcome in and of itself. It's a helpful tailwind that assists your efforts. To take full advantage of it, you must first set a destination point.

———

A year is longer than you think. A lot can happen in that time, and the things that can occur are not limited to money. Some people study hard and get into the school they want, while others manage to grow their business by working with dedication.

We make a choice, we take responsibility, and we focus. We repeat that scheme until the day we die. That's what life is about. It's a cycle that's inexorably linked to free will. The only variables are whether you made a good or bad choice and how dedicated you were to it.

What choice you make and how much effort you invest in it ultimately depend on your willpower. Your intention has the power to make the difference between success and failure. To do nothing and still expect a lucky break, as Simon did, is the equivalent of asking for top grades when you haven't written a single word on the paper called life.

This is what I tell people who ask, "Why do I have such bad luck?" instead of putting their good fortune to use while they have it.

Think of luck as air mileage points. Air miles come with an expiration date, after which you lose them. Are you going to let them go to waste? Of course not. The wise thing to do is to take advantage while you can, as much as you can. When you come across good luck, you need to take action to make the most of it while you have it and before it expires.

You may have heard the expression "ten-year-long luck."[*] Long luck is ten years, short luck is five, and minor luck is one. Dividing time into shorter periods allows us to see the general direction of fortune's flow.

I often advise people to focus on the idea of the minor

---

[*] Ship (ten) nyeon (year) dae (great) woon (fortune).

luck available to all at the lunar new year that begins after Ip-chun.* To imagine making use of the minor luck available to all at that time can feel less overwhelming than trying to visualize a scenario of good fortune that's ten years long. That would feel like you are facing a huge, unclimbable wall. In contrast, "this year's luck" is renewed every year, which allows everyone to have a fresh start. It is a moment in time when there is plenty of space for you to intervene by using this year's luck to add energy to your objectives, even if it doesn't change the overall course of events.

Beginning the year with a clean slate every spring at Ip-chun has the benefit of lifting your spirits, too. Action is key. Your intentions and your choices shape your behavior, and the sum of your actions will be reflected in your fortune that year.

Nobody knows what's going to happen in life, not even a single month into the future. This is especially true in today's world, where change only seems to accelerate. If you feel like one year is long, then it means there is enough time for you to make a change or steer your ship in a different direction.

You must envision your luck clearly and decide what ac-

---

* Korea traditionally follows the lunar calendar, which includes twenty-four solar terms called Jeolgi. These Jeolgis split the year into different seasons according to weather and climate, with each spaced approximately fifteen days apart. The observance of these Jeolgis was highly important in Korea in predicting agricultural cycles and observing other seasonal rituals. Ip-chun was a very important day in the lunar calendar, with many rituals held on this day to help ensure successful farming that year. The Chinese characters for the word *Ip-chun*, meaning "start of spring," were traditionally written on rectangular signs and hung above household doorways to bring good luck (gastrotourseoul.com).

tions you're going to take. The best luck in the world will disappear into thin air if you ignore it.

Even now, as you read this, your luck is hoping to catch your attention and grow to its fullest. What will you do with it?

Are Samjae* and the Nine Years Phenomenon Important to Consider?

In traditional Korean folklore and divinatory rituals as well as in Buddhism, the numbers three and nine have important meanings. "The three years of misfortune" is a Korean belief that disasters come to all of us, and that they often come in sets of threes. Samjae is the Buddhist concept of the "three (sam) disasters (jae)." The word *sam-jae* (pronounced *sahm-jae*) describes the three disasters that occur in an interval of nine years. The first year is called deul-sam-jae (the incoming three disasters), the second nul-sam-jae (the settling three disasters), and the third nal-sam-jae (the outgoing three disasters). Among all three, deulsamjae is the harshest.

In Korea, whenever someone is hit by misfortune, people tend to ascribe it to samjae. By that logic, half of humanity should be struck by unexpected misfortune at any one time.

But I want to underline that samjae is not always a bad

* Samjae are "the Three Disasters" in Buddhism, or the "three years of misfortune" according to Korean folklore and traditional divinatory practice.

thing. As I have already written elsewhere in this book, a time of crisis can be an opportunity in disguise and can lead to a happy ending. That's why people have created the expressions *bok-sam-jae* (lucky samjae) for when things turn out positively and *ak-sam-jae* (unlucky samjae) for the opposite case.

The Nine Years Phenomenon or "nine-ender" is no different. Nine comes right before ten, the number of completeness in Korean tradition. So the attributes of the number nine are thought to be something to be very cautious about, as nine is considered a time of change and instability—in short, bad luck. In Korea, a "nine-ender" does not mean a chronological year that ends in nine, like 1999 or 2009, but designates a person's age that ends in nine, such as twenty-nine, thirty-nine, or forty-nine. Thus, it is considered necessary to avoid major life decisions such as marriage, childbirth, starting a business, or moving when an individual is in a nine year. For example, advice may be given such as "Postpone marriage at twenty-nine," or "Don't start a new business at thirty-nine." Of course, there are many people these days who do not follow such advice.

It is similar to how Koreans view the change in seasons. During the "interseasons," periods filled with instability and turmoil before a new season begins, luck is also felt to be less powerful. But like samjae, if you attune yourself to these periods of change and instability and try to see how you can capitalize on them, they may turn out to be beneficial.

In a nutshell, in my experience, samjae and the phenomenon of the nines are real, but some people may be impacted while others may not. When you find yourself in those potentially unlucky periods, try to keep calm and act cautiously to avert bad fortune. Ideally, when those periods are over, you will be able to tell yourself, *That went better than I'd expected*, or *That was not that big a deal.*

If you don't already know your Chinese zodiac sign, you will want to look it up on one of the many sites online that can tell you. Once you know your animal sign, you can use the table below to learn when to expect your samjae based on your Chinese zodiac sign.

CHINESE ZODIAC SIGN	SNAKE ROOSTER OX	MONKEY RAT DRAGON	PIG RABBIT SHEEP	TIGER HORSE DOG
DEULSAMJAE	Year of the Pig	Year of the Tiger	Year of the Snake	Year of the Monkey
NULSAMJAE	Year of the Rat	Year of the Rabbit	Year of the Horse	Year of the Rooster
NALSAMJAE	Year of the Ox	Year of the Dragon	Year of the Sheep	Year of the Dog

The Psychology of
SELF-SUGGESTION

3

Opportunities Find Those Who Can Decipher the Future

FEEL THE PULSE OF YOUR INTUITION

"How on earth did you find out?"

"I knew you would do something like that."

There are some things you just "know," like when your boyfriend is cheating on you. It doesn't matter if your feelings are your only evidence. You may want to dismiss it as nonsense, but let's say such things are possible for the sake of this argument. I've noticed a common quality in people who are successful in the entertainment business. They all have gut feelings or hunches. They're the type of people who make statements like, "Anna is guaranteed to win first place," or,

"This new weekend drama is going to be a huge success," even from the very beginning and then turn out to be right.

It's hard to find anyone successful in the entertainment business who lacks this sort of intuition, especially performers. Singers are a good example. Their onstage personas often have nothing to do with who they are in real life. It's as if they switch personalities when the camera turns on. When I started working in entertainment and witnessed people transform into mesmerizing singers before my eyes as soon as they were on stage, I wondered, *How is that possible?* But people with good instincts spot that sort of talent long before the performer themselves can see it.

Once I entered the world of luck, I understood. There is something you can't explain logically, a voice that whispers, *I don't know why, but this is how things are going to be.* That feeling, called intuition, is the key to success and is highly developed in wealthy people. Rich people are particularly good at predicting events a few steps ahead. They instantly sense how a particular situation will play out and devise a brilliant way to make money off it.

In that sense, investing is very much about intuition. Nobody knows whether the stock they bought today will turn into gold or a piece of junk, but rich people trust their intuition and are confident in their choices. Legendary investors' ability to see ten years into the future is not mere guesswork.

———•

In the 1860s, an American doctor named James Caleb Jackson noticed that a diet of vegetables and water helped his patients recover from various illnesses. Based on this observation, he developed a health food made with whole grains and water that he called Granula. Made of simple, unprocessed ingredients, his creation originally piqued the public's interest thanks to its health benefits. Unfortunately, Jackson's Granula was too hard to chew and, most crucially, tasteless. Nobody wanted to eat it, not even patients who were in urgent need of recovery.

That's when the Kellogg brothers, John Harvey and Will Keith, who worked at the hospital with Jackson, had a lightbulb moment and tried different ways to make his creation more palatable. After much trial and error, they decided to make thin flakes after rolling out the dough. The world's most popular cereal brand, Kellogg's, was born. The cornflakes flew off the shelves, bringing the Kellogg brothers immense wealth and fame.

This story teaches us something important: the power of intuition. If the Kellogg brothers hadn't thought that Granula could be profitable, if they had only seen its drawbacks and not its tremendous potential for success, would they have gained all of their wealth?

Great intuition is a mysterious power that allows you to

instantly understand and manifest your goals. Some people refer to it as the "resolution of the mind." It's like taking a photo with a high-resolution camera, so the picture comes out sharp and vivid.

———

Koreans are remarkably intuitive. Just look at the number of medals in international competitions like archery, shooting, golf, and fencing. Watching the Korean national archery team, known as shin-goong,[*] you'll see that no matter how many points the opponents get or regardless of the wind dynamics, the athletes don't get flustered. Another example is Korean mothers. Unlike restaurant chefs, they seldom rely on recipes. They cook with instinct rather than precision, yet their food hits the spot. What these examples show is that intuition is closely linked to highly evolved sensory perception—the subtle shifts in the wind on the archery range, or the big difference a small change in seasoning can have on a dish. Scientific and industrial development emphasize logic and reason. But in recent years, there has been an increased interest on the other end of the spectrum: emotions, sensations, and intuition.

A part of intuition is innate to all of us. Nevertheless, successful people constantly train their intuition. They intently

---

[*] A ghostlike or spirit-like bow; by extension a great archer.

watch and listen to the world around them from an early age. They accumulate as much experience as they can, which leads to a balanced development of the left and right parts of their brain. By doing so, they build an emotional logic that acts as the basis for their own development.

They use that intuitive power to unearth opportunities and turn them into money. People say the fourth industrial era will be the era of the spiritual quotient (SQ). That ability is on a different level from IQ (intelligence quotient) or EQ (emotional quotient). The greatest AI (artificial intelligence) in the world cannot replace it, as it belongs to the kind of mental dimension only humans can develop at the deepest levels.

A woman's hunch that her boyfriend is cheating on her is no accident. She noticed the small lies he repeatedly told her and that he was often late for their date nights. Those subtle clues and the sum of her sensory experiences—his voice, his tone, the look in his eyes—all constitute evidence that pointed to his change of heart. Ultimately, her intuition helped her make the right choice: to break up for her own happiness.

There are no accidents in the world. You can make money and shape the future if you watch and listen to the world around you and know how to read the flow of the moment.

RICH PEOPLE ALWAYS CARRY MONEY

The man was impeccably dressed, every button scrupulously fastened. He had the unmistakable air of an educator. Now in his mid-fifties, he entered the private education market in the 1990s and has since built a private academy empire worth ten million dollars.

"Are you taking notes right now?" I asked him.

"Yes, I keep them close in case I need them. It's a habit," he replied.

I was intrigued by this well-to-do man holding a pen in his hand and writing down what I was saying. People with high social standing usually let other people's advice go in one ear and out the other.

Some of the people I've met have been like that. You can advise them in the most honest way you can, but they will only take in and respond to what they like and ignore anything they don't. They get irritated by the idea that anyone would dare try to tell them what to do. By comparison, the older gentleman in front of me was as attentive as a model student.

"Do you always take notes so assiduously?" I asked.

He replied, "Yes, if I think it's helpful. If a good sentence, a lesson, or a feeling occurs, I write it down, even if it's not relevant right then and there. I always find opportunities to use them. In fact, my notes have served me well for my classes and when I was expanding my business."

I was captivated by the gentleman's life story. After repeatedly failing the qualifying exam, he had given up on becoming a schoolteacher and started teaching as a tutor at a private after-school institute. He loved teaching, but a private tutor was not a highly admired occupation back then. All of his friends from college had become certified schoolteachers, while he kept moving from one academy to another.

In the beginning, he was preoccupied with making ends meet. Then, he came to terms with the fact that the only way forward was to become the best tutor he could be. That's when he started writing everything down as if he were possessed. Every story was valuable material as long as it helped him attract more students and teach them well.

At first, he focused on keeping his students interested. He wanted the kids to have something to laugh about, something that could distract them from their daily routine. Next, he incorporated humor into math formulas so his students could memorize them a little more easily.

It wasn't long before word of mouth spread among the parents. It took him three years to go from a competent tutor to the most renowned instructor in the area. A few more years later, he became the CEO of a conglomerate of multiple academies.

This is what he told me: "I have piles and piles of notebooks at home. I keep them all. Sometimes I get comments like 'Oh, that must be cumbersome!' but I feel like they're a part of me now. I can't leave the house without my pen and notebook, lest I miss noting down an important idea. The mere thought of not having my notebook makes me anxious."

Indeed, he's never stopped taking notes, even after he became so successful. Whether he was attending an educational forum, meeting a casual acquaintance, or participating in an important business meeting, he always carried his notebook with him. To this day, his notes from the daily news or conversations with people are a useful tool that help him stay at the top of his game.

His college friends no longer laugh at him. Instead, they envy his life as a multimillionaire.

In the end, we shape our lives with our own hands. I always pay close attention to the behavior of people who seek my advice. Some are poor, and some are rich, but there is one thing I can definitely tell from their attitude. Successful people behave differently from ordinary people, even when it comes to receiving something. They look at me with a sparkle in their eyes, pin back their ears, and actively write down what I say. In short, they shrewdly take what they need without missing a crumb. And even if they don't use them right away, they keep and chew on those notes until the moment arrives when they can build their luck with them.

It doesn't matter if it's something that doesn't have much meaning or depth at the time. The act of taking notes itself is filled with the desire to succeed and the will to bend fate in one's favor. Recording information to be used later can not only fill the gaps in one's luck, but also can be used as a stepping stone to the changes that can bring about prosperity.

HOW TO ROLL THE DICE WITH SEED MONEY

Wealthy people are not only good at making money; they're good at keeping it, too. It makes you wonder whether it's easier to keep money than to earn it or if there is a secret trick that prevents money from leaving your hands once you have it.

I interned at a TV station when I was in college. At the time, you could meet a lot of celebrities on set even if you weren't a more senior person like a writer or producer. Some of the celebrities I met included middle-aged broadcasters who had become property owners after years of working and up-and-coming actors who had just been propelled to stardom by a single film. It's hard to know what these people are truly like when you only see their perfectly crafted appearance on the big or small screen. Even so, there is one place where you can get a glimpse of their genuine selves, and that's at the dinner table.

One day, I was just finishing shooting an entertainment show where I spent most of my working hours running from task to task. I was a college intern who had just turned twenty, and I was catching my breath after a particularly rough day when a highly renowned senior broadcaster approached me.

"Today was pretty hard, wasn't it? You must be exhausted."

They must have felt bad for the young intern I was. They suddenly handed me an envelope filled with cash, which felt quite thick in my hands. I stood there for a while, not knowing what to do. How could I refuse a gesture of kindness from a respected senior? At the time, I accepted it as a sign of encouragement and got back to work with uplifted spirits.

As it turned out, that senior broadcaster was successful for a reason. They were as great in person as their public-facing persona. What caught my attention, nevertheless, was their wallet. It was neat, well-aged, and filled with cash. Of course, I wasn't the only one they had shown kindness to. They would always give some pocket money to the younger staff members or use that cash to pay for company dinners.

———•———

A decade later, I encountered several people who resembled that senior broadcaster. Their elegantly tanned leather wallets contained bills organized by denomination. I realize the expression "thick wallet" must feel somewhat out of place in today's cashless society. Of course, those people used electronic payment services, too, in special situations where large sums of money were involved, such as land sales, real estate transactions, and new business contracts. However, they always carried a certain amount of cash in their wallet every day as if it were a protective amulet. This included 10,000-won ($7 USD) and 50,000-won ($35 USD) bills with images of King

Sejong the Great[*] and Shin Saimdang,[†] respectively, as well as 1,000-won (75¢ USD) bills with Yi Hwang.[‡]

When you're that rich, you probably don't even need to carry around any cash, I thought to myself. They must have assistants and housekeepers, so they don't have to go out and pay for things themselves. I didn't understand why they still carried bills in their wallets.

However, I realized that for the superrich I've met, directly and indirectly, the meaning of cash surpassed its monetary value. By seeing and touching cash, they maintain a tangible contact with money, which is something you can't do with stocks or Bitcoins because their value is virtual and, therefore, invisible.

There are other reasons why wealthy people always carry cash with them. When you pay for valet parking or want to thank a server or hairdresser for their kindness, you can't just ask them for their account number. But if you have cash in your wallet, you can take it out at a moment's notice and express your gratitude whenever you want. Repaying a favor you've received requires a kind heart, but it's also a source of

---

[*] The fourth king of the Joseon dynasty (reigned 1418–1450) and the creator of Hangul, the Korean alphabet.

[†] A Korean artist, writer, calligraphist, and poet, often held up as a model of Confucian ideals. She is the first and only woman to date to appear on a South Korean banknote.

[‡] A sixteenth-century Confucian scholar, also known as Toegye.

appeasement and gratitude to the universe when given by the wealthy.

It's not uncommon to find wealthy people who like to physically touch and feel money to keep their "sense of money" alive. It's often particularly noticeable in people who do business on a large scale.

There is a famous bakery in Korea that the same family has run for three generations. The bakery is located in a small provincial town, but it generates a few hundred thousand dollars in sales . . . daily. The bakery has turned the entire city into a tourist attraction. The owners bought a building that they converted into a store, which hundreds, even thousands of customers crowd into daily to buy bread. The business is doing so well that the employees don't have a minute to breathe. Bills and coins flow in and out of the cash register that is constantly opening and closing.

Amid all that rush, a person stands at the entrance every day and watches over the scene. It's the founder, who first opened the bakery. Until a few years ago, he was at the original store every day, all day long. At first, even the locals who frequented the store regularly didn't know who he was. It was only later, as the business became popular, that people recognized his face from the local newspaper. As I watched him, I realized: He wasn't watching the cash register; he was studying the flow of money.

Every neighborhood has its iconic restaurants, those businesses large enough to be considered landmarks. From the multistory giant wang-galbi restaurant in Suwon to the original tteok-galbi* restaurant that went viral in Damyang, the founders of successful restaurants with monthly sales amounting to hundreds of millions of won all stand behind their counters religiously.

It's one of the distinguishing characteristics of people with a flair for business, those who are exceptionally resourceful. If you're a regular office worker whose paycheck just passes through your bank account, you never get to touch your money. When a number appears in your bank account, it means you've received a payment, and when the number decreases, it means you've spent money, so the concept of "money" is just numbers that appear and disappear into thin air. Meanwhile, trendy investments such as stocks and crypto are all about moving from this number to that or the number going up and down. In short, you can't "feel" the flow of money through its touch, weight, or texture.

It's not surprising that the people who touch cash the most are the ones who see the flow of money and feel the pulse of the business faster and more accurately. Only those who can see, touch, and feel the flow of cash can strengthen their intuition about money.

---

* A Korean dish that consists of short rib (galbi in Korean) beef patties seasoned with a sweet and savory sauce. It is called tteok-galbi because the rib (galbi) is minced and pounded like tteok (rice cake), which makes it tender and easy to digest. The name wang-galbi refers to the "jumbo" size of the meat, which is about three to five times bigger than typical galbi pieces.

—•—

Here's an easy example. You live in an apartment for which you pay a monthly rent of seven hundred dollars, which is paid electronically every month. One day, your transactions are interrupted by a computer failure. You are forced to hand over seven hundred dollars in cash to your landlord. Even if it's the same amount, it feels different somehow. Think about the lightness of seven hundred dollars you send by swiping a screen with your finger and the heaviness of seven hundred dollars' worth of bills you hold in your hand, feeling their weight and volume through your fingers.

This is how huge the difference is between what's visible and what's invisible, even for the same amount of money. If you don't use cash and only make online purchases, it's easy to get used to seeing numbers and forget the real weight and value of money.

That's what motivates rich people to carry cash. Rich people all have a basic fear of money. The moment they lose their grip on it, they run the risk of making a mistake or getting caught up in a complicated situation that could lead to signif-icant losses. That's why they always keep cash on hand, even if it's only a small amount. It's a good way to maintain your sense of money that helps you accumulate wealth.

I don't know about other countries, but in Korea, you never give an empty wallet as a present. You usually put a few banknotes inside to wish the person good luck with money and that their wallet will get filled. As the saying goes, smiling brings good fortune, and carrying money attracts good luck. It doesn't have to be a lot; a few bills can be a great seed to grow into a fortune. That is how rich people slowly accumulate their wealth, one bill at a time.

THE FUTURE BELONGS TO THOSE WHO DECIPHER IT FIRST

Launching a new television show is always a gamble. Production costs alone can be hundreds of thousands of dollars per episode, and so many people depend on the show for their livelihoods. It's a hit-or-miss, all-or-nothing business. Of course, getting high ratings makes everyone happy. When that happens, as an employee, you would get incentives and additional days off. If you stayed long enough and the show remained successful, you would even be guaranteed a fast-track promotion. But what if the opposite happens? There can't be anything worse than that. The risk of a flop is far greater than the benefits of a hit.

Live broadcasting, in particular, is an all-consuming process. Creating a show that appeals to viewers means destroying your peace of mind by your own choice. That's how intense live television is. The mere thought of an accident during a live broadcast was enough to freeze my mind and make me dizzy, not to mention the fear of massive disappointment from the audience and a severe reprimand from my bosses.

I wondered why I was having such a hard time even though I was living the life of my dreams. I suddenly felt a huge wave of admiration for the celebrities who came in and smiled for the camera every single day, no matter how they were actually feeling.

———

Chloe was a comedian who had recently risen in popularity. I was sitting with a gloomy look on my face during a break when she approached me and asked if something was going on with me. After exchanging some small talk, I asked her: "Doesn't all of this make you anxious? There is no guarantee of success; it's all a big gamble. I know celebrities who have to take sleeping pills because they get so nervous before a show. I get that this is how this world works, but how are you supposed to stay calm when you can't see an inch ahead?"

Chloe calmly watched me fret, then answered: "I don't worry at all. If I don't believe in myself, who will? Even the most confident people have a hard time making it, so imagine the result without any faith in yourself. That kind of negativity is not going to get you anywhere."

She was right. Thanks to her spirited rhetoric, Chloe had managed to survive in the jungle that is the Korean entertainment industry. In her ten-year career, she had gone through all sorts of twists and turns, earning herself both the love of the public and big money. And now she was telling me it was her faith that led her to success? Honestly, I felt dispirited. I was expecting some extraordinary secret to be behind all her accomplishments.

Now years later, I understand what she meant. I've read the fortunes of countless people and realized the successful ones share something in common. It's a word that's so overused it's almost lost its meaning: belief. Every person I've met who could call themselves "successful" viewed and treated themselves in a different way from the average individual. They were willfully giving themselves the kind of unlimited belief that you can only grant yourself.

———•———

Interestingly, the rich also know how to turn this type of self-belief into successful action. It's called "self-suggestion." One entrepreneur who enjoyed massive success through their scented-candle business had this to say about self-suggestion:

"I don't trust anyone, only myself."

"How is that possible? Is there anything special you do to promote trust in yourself?"

"It's nothing big, really, but I have this morning routine. I say what I want to happen out loud. That's it. I voice what I envision to myself. Something like, 'I'm getting closer to being someone who can have anything' or 'Today is another day I am working toward success.' You know, that kind of thing."

"And do you feel that it makes a difference?" I asked.

"Yes. They may seem like simple sentences without much meaning, but they have an undeniable impact. I was skeptical, too, at first, but even if there is no scientific argument to prove it, just saying those words out loud has a psychological effect. When I vocalize what I want to be, I feel like my actions and thoughts become more aligned with that objective. Anyway, I think that's what helps me with my business and relationship."

They had a point. Statements like "I can be successful" and "I can be rich" are extremely vague. They may seem positive and uplifting, but they don't give you any direction on how to get there.

However, saying "I'm getting closer to . . ." or "I'm moving toward . . ." is different. It clearly shows your sense of purpose and the effort you are making every day to reach your goal.

In retrospect, I realized that more people made use of self-suggestion than I had thought. That was the case with Chloe, who cheered me on during a break. She was practicing self-suggestion, although she hadn't made it a daily routine. She must have told countless people, "Don't worry, everything is going to be okay," throughout the day. And every time, Chloe was the first person to hear that message and remember it.

International gold medal–winning athletes are no exception. In the fencing final at the Rio Olympics, Park Sangyoung was down nine to thirteen. As he was losing, he was seen mumbling to himself as if to cast a spell. He later said he had heard the crowd cheering him and repeated the words "I can do this" to himself. He then pulled himself together and fought back to defeat his opponent fifteen to fourteen, clinching the gold. He had flipped the outcome by changing his attitude.

— ·

The self-made wealthy are another category of people whom I have discovered use all sorts of similar methods. Some keep a mantra in their wallet that they regularly take out to read, while others outline what they want their life to become within the next year every night before sleep. It could be a single sentence that sets a goal, the face of someone they aspire to be like, or a mental image they want to remember. Whatever it is, the desire for money and success is the same. No matter how strong your desire is, keeping it to yourself is not going to yield any results. You have to take it out of your body by speaking it or writing it, even if it's only for yourself. That's what will stir your body in that direction.

When I only believed in things I could see, I thought self-suggestion practice was some sort of game. Entering the invisible world of luck led me to respect each person's beliefs for what they are. If you firmly believe in something, someone else's belief may seem fake to you. But that means that your belief can also appear to be fake in the eyes of another person.

I used to doubt whether there was such a thing as complete trust, but now I know. I've learned that people can have 100 percent faith in something and that it can bring greater success than you could ever imagine. I've also learned that luck will never come near a person who doesn't know how to value themselves and treats themselves accordingly. It goes without saying that everything related to money works the same way.

THE MIDNIGHT PRAYER: THE PRAYER OF THE RICH

"How can I attract good luck?"

This is a question that people have asked me endlessly ever since I started reading fortunes. And there is one suggestion I invariably make: the prayer at the Hour of the Rat, or "midnight prayer."

The response is usually something like this: "What's that? You should know, I'm not religious."

To which I give a simple explanation: "It doesn't matter. What's important is that you wish yourself well because you are the one praying."

The "Hour of the Rat" indicates the time between eleven p.m. and one a.m. In ancient times, people named the hours of the day after animals. They divided the twenty-four hours of a day into two-hour periods and named them after the twelve animals of the Chinese zodiac, also known as the twelve Earthly Branches.[*] Each period is associated with the times of day when the corresponding animal is active, with the first hour being the Hour of the Rat. Although we no longer use terms like *chuk-shi* (the Hour of the Ox) or *myo-shi* (the Hour of the Rabbit), we still refer to the twelve hours between eleven a.m. and one p.m. as "noon,"[†] which corresponds to oh-shi (the Hour of the Horse), and the two hours between eleven p.m. and one a.m. as "midnight,"[‡] which corresponds to ja-shi (the Hour of the Rat).

Now, how do you go about it? To start with, you need to have a specific length of time in mind or even a format for how you will pray. It is recommended that you pray at midnight to amplify your luck. According to the Chinese zodiac system, the Hour of the Rat is a time of transition, the time when today ends and tomorrow begins. It's a time when you can calm down and concentrate. If you pray at a time when you are not distracted and at your most focused, the results are bound to be quick and certain.

———

Traditionally, when praying, it's common to call on someone to address your prayers to, like God or Buddha, but a typical

---

[*] Each Earthly Branch is associated with an animal: rat, ox, tiger, rabbit, dragon, snake, horse, sheep, monkey, rooster, dog, or pig.
[†] Jeong-oh in Korean, which translates to "the middle of (the Hour of) the Horse."
[‡] Ja-jeong in Korean, which translates to "the middle of (the Hour of) the Rat."

midnight prayer has no divine subject. A midnight prayer is a prayer to yourself. If you're religious, you can pray to the god you believe in. The important thing is that you focus on yourself as the subject of the prayer. It's not God who hears your prayers, and it's not God who will eventually respond to them. The midnight prayer is a special act rooted in good intentions for yourself.

The process is quite simple. First, identify yourself: "My name is ______."

Next, describe your current situation in detail, followed by a clear statement of what you want to accomplish. Most importantly, you must speak up.

"But why do you have to say it out loud?"

"I can just write it down in my journal, can't I?"

Many people react with skepticism. However, having experienced the effectiveness of prayer myself, I answer with conviction.

"Yes, that's what most people do. But keeping a journal involves a lot of hiding and deception. Handwriting can't keep up with the speed of thought, and you end up leaving out many things because you're trying to edit the content of your mind. When you say it out loud, on the other hand, your genuine thoughts pour directly out of your mouth, unfiltered. This way, you gain a clearer perspective than you can through any other method."

"Is that why you have to say your name?"

"That's right. Reaffirming who you are has an impact on your mindset. You pray about your situation and state your wishes with a clear knowledge of who you are, which is what allows you to see things as they are and move forward."

"Oh, so it's a prayer I say for myself."

"Exactly."

A few words of advice before you do the midnight prayer: Make sure your situation and purpose are well defined. It can't be winning the lottery, getting one million dollars, or becoming rich. Prayer only works if you wish for something specific and realistic, such as an event that will likely occur soon.

Every night during the Hour of the Rat, calmly say your prayer before you go to bed. After six months, write down your prayer verbatim. As you write it, check to see if the situation has changed or the prayer has been fulfilled.

Someone asked me another question about the prayer: "Why do you write it down after six months instead of from the beginning?"

I replied: "To examine what you've realized. You write down the situation and the wishes that you told yourself in your own voice for the past six months. If anything has changed at all, write a comment on the bottom: how the situation has changed, if your wish has come true, and so on. If it didn't work out, repeat the prayer and check back in after six more months. Don't just talk about difficult situations or problems you're facing. You have to draw an outline for the next step you're going to take. 'I' am the one praying, and 'I' am the one listening."

———

Keith was in a tricky situation at work. He was having trouble coping with the excessive workload. After confessing his difficulty in his midnight prayers, he expressed his personal wishes for change. He asked for a transfer from his current team or the opportunity to move to another job. Six months later, Keith opened his notebook and wrote down his prayer. Underneath, he wrote the outcome for each situation and each wish. To his surprise, he noticed a change in his daily routine as he continued to say his prayers.

Keith was working more than the legal eight-hour workday for office workers. Through prayer, he realized that overwork was his biggest problem, and he subconsciously made small steps to resolve that issue. First, he calculated his monthly working hours and reported his overtime to his boss. He also shared that his workload was too much for one person to handle. His actions brought about change. His boss arranged for him to share his work with a colleague to lessen his burden. That alone gave Keith some breathing room.

In the meantime, Keith continued working on personal

development and looking for opportunities to change jobs. He studied English regularly and became proficient enough to be hired by another company if he still wanted to move. However, informing his employer of the situation had already cut his workload in half, so he decided to stay at his current company, where there was no shortage of opportunities for him to use his English skills.

What if Keith had just complained about his situation without understanding it? Perhaps he would still be lamenting his fate, resigned to go to work every day, feeling like he had no other choice. That would have been bad for Keith and bad for the company.

Look how different life can be once you correctly perceive your situation. The same goes for money.

———•———

Lena was an office worker who hadn't gotten a raise in years. She was paid on the twenty-fifth of each month, but her bank balance was always negative. She doubted whether she would ever be able to afford to buy a home. With rising mortgage rates and inflation, a flat salary was synonymous with a pay cut. In a time when "everything goes up except your salary," her income was stagnating, and her investments weren't growing in the stock market. Lena was giving up on the hope of ever becoming rich, let alone comfortable.

Nevertheless, she told me that hearing my advice about the

midnight prayer made her feel like she had nothing to lose, so she started praying. Every night at midnight, she would join her hands and specifically ask for more money than she had now.

This was her prayer six months ago:

Subject: *"My name is Lena."*

Situation: *"The cost of living keeps increasing, but my salary hasn't changed. I'm worried I'm not saving enough money."*

Wish: *"I want to find a side job I can do regardless of the time."*

This is the prayer she wrote in her notebook and the changes that occurred six months later:

Subject: *"My name is Lena."*

Situation: *"The cost of living keeps increasing, but my salary hasn't changed. I'm worried I'm not saving enough money."*

- *I figured out my company's average annual salary increase and focused on improving my sales performance. My performance in the second quarter was good, so I got a bonus.*

Wish: *"I want to find a side job I can do regardless of the time."*

* *I opened an online marketplace and organized group purchases. I sold them with a small margin and earned some extra income.*

Through prayer, Lena realized the only way to make money was to either earn more or spend less. First, she looked at her company's annual salary increase rate. There wasn't much hope there, so she dedicated herself to improving her work performance instead. It wasn't much, but she still got a bonus for her efforts in the second quarter. She parked all that unexpected income in an installment savings account without spending a penny.

Lena also started thinking about other ways to generate income outside her salary and what she could do after work to realize her goal. She had a blog where she documented her daily life, mainly to an audience of young women who showed particular interest in the face masks and cosmetics she used. That gave her an idea.

"I know! I'm going to open an online marketplace."

She started introducing cosmetic products she found effective on her blog and organizing joint purchases for a small profit. Of course, she didn't make a lot of money from the get-go, but generating income outside her day job gave her a great sense of accomplishment and confidence.

Praying with a clear assessment of her situation made a big difference for Lena. She belatedly experienced the effectiveness of midnight prayers firsthand and thanked me for it. She says she never misses a single prayer, that it has become a natural habit for her. Now that she's seen the benefits, she strives to make the prayer as specific as possible.

When she considers the prayers as an action with an immediate effect rather than something that is already part of the past, she can feel her mind clear. She says her name in a clear voice, describes her situation in detail, and then prays fervently. She prays every day for six months. Then, she writes in her notebook, hoping to confirm her heartfelt prayer has been fulfilled, as if by magic.

Whatever problem you're facing, the first thing to do is recognize your exact situation. You could say that, in that regard, midnight prayers are a tool you can use to work things out yourself rather than a request for the heavens to answer.

THE UPWARD SPIRAL, OR WHY YOU MUST EXPERIENCE SUCCESS TO ACHIEVE SUCCESS

There was an entrepreneur who had made a fortune starting a health juice business on her own, but her business quickly ran into trouble. A slew of brands with similar concepts sprung up like mushrooms after the rain, increasing the competition and eroding her profit margins. The more her business declined, the more distressed she became. The circumstances brought her to have her fortune read rather frequently.

One day, she declared she was stepping away from the business for a while. She wanted to figure out how to move forward and, most importantly, take some time to recover from the shock of her failure. She had been in a lot of pain, spending sleepless nights investigating the decline in sales of her business. I didn't see her for a while after that.

Almost half a year had gone by when I saw her again. Her expression had brightened considerably. The dark circles had disappeared, and her eyes overflowed with motivation. Her cheeks were no longer hollow and had a healthy glow. I knew she had pulled herself out of her bad spell.

Before I could even ask her, she started to speak.

"I've started something new," she said, "I'm revamping the stores."

"You're back in business? That's great to hear! I thought you wouldn't be back for a while."

"No, not at all. I was practicing 'being successful.' Every single day."

That's why she looked so much better. The rest of her story was captivating.

For a long while after the decline of her stores, she had been deeply depressed. She felt like she was going to fail no matter what she did. She rushed to the gym near her house before her depression swallowed her whole, where she discovered she had more strength than she realized.

She started to work out for the first time in her life. At first, she struggled to lift one-pound dumbbells. After she'd built some muscle, however, the weights began to feel incredibly light, and soon, she was able to lift five pounds with no trouble. The physical effort was tough to bear, but the feeling of accomplishment was exhilarating. After experiencing gradual success, she was able to gather her spirits again and resume her business.

After remodeling the stores based on a new strategy that set her apart from other brands, she proposed new menus blending a variety of tropical fruits that proved highly successful with younger customers. By achieving small victories every day through exercise, the entrepreneur was preparing for a bigger success.

—•—

Of course, the opposite is possible, too. A senior manager working at a conglomerate once came to me for advice. He was feeling extremely overwhelmed and anxious after being assigned a new project, right after he had been passed over for promotion once again. He had to spend an increasing amount of money on private tutoring as his children grew. His endlessly ballooning expenses reminded him all the time of his stagnating position in the company. Even if he didn't make it to the highest ranks, he thought he would feel so much more at peace if he at least got a promotion. With a higher basic salary and a performance bonus, he could expect at least a 9 percent raise.

The manager had been on a downward spiral for several years. Still, I saw he had a good chance to climb out of this dark pit if he just managed to get through that year. With that positive picture in mind, I gave him some honest advice.

"You'll have better luck, soon."

"Sorry?"

"Just make sure you take advantage of whatever opportunities come your way. You've got to give it your all; if you do, things will turn around for you."

"I . . . do you think I can make it?"

"Of course. Let me know if you have any good news."

The man quivered as he listened. Then he headed home, a miserable expression on his face.

I heard back from him as the new year started. He somehow sounded very quiet.

Later, I couldn't help but feel sorry for him when I heard what had happened. Apparently, he had felt more worried than excited to hear his luck would improve. He doubted whether he could lead the project to success single-handedly, as he had never achieved anything on his own before.

This wasn't surprising. Self-improvement was not his

strong suit. He was always late for work, never put in more energy than everyone else did, and spent the day with his head down until it was time to go home. Working his way up from junior employee to senior manager had not been too hard; he had just been given different titles as his seniority built up over time. In short, he hadn't worked his way up the ladder. All he had done was just keep showing up.

Now his fears had become reality. Having never experienced any success of his own making, the manager failed at his new project. His chance for promotion had vanished entirely.

———•———

The man's story taught me something. You have to experience success to achieve success. From my intuition when meeting with the manager, it was obvious good luck was waiting for him. But no matter how great your luck may be, it's meaningless if you don't manage to grab it. Some people seize good fortune and make it their own, while others miss it altogether or let themselves be crushed by it.

Where does that ability to grab your luck come from? In the same way the entrepreneur had pulled herself out of bad luck through exercise, you build the power to seize success just like you build muscle strength. While big successes are often as unreachable as the stars in the sky, small successes are infinite and very much within reach. They just require a little effort.

In fact, we experience success every day. Waking up to the

first alarm in the morning is a success, as is getting to work on time and completing the tasks assigned to you for the day. Thanks to these small, repeated victories, we get closer to success all the time. But we need to notice those successes and remind ourselves of them so that when we are presented with larger challenges and opportunities, we have the confidence to grab them.

That's why it doesn't matter if a success is small. It doesn't have to be a big deal. It could be reading an article about the economy every evening, losing a pound every month, or baking delicious cookies for your family on the weekend. What matters is that you experience small, consistent successes and praise yourself for them. Then, eventually, you will realize, just as I did, that it's not luck that makes you successful; it's success that makes you lucky.

Wealthy, successful people are much more diligent than you might think. Even now, they're accumulating wins, big and small, to become even more successful while others aren't even making an attempt to try.

DOES STRENGTH OF CHARACTER EQUAL SUCCESS?

At one time or another, we've all thought that successful people aren't ordinary. If they got rich so quickly, they must have done something differently. Most people think something like this, with only slight variations in the nuance:

They must be the worst person in the world.

No doubt, they have no heart.

Rich people are often portrayed as having a temper or being difficult to deal with. In fact, some say that you can't get rich with a soft, marshmallow-like mindset. But does the same rule apply to the world of luck? At least for the rich people I know in my world, the word *gi*[*] is used to describe inner strength of a completely different nature.

———•———

Alex was a musician who had reached the pinnacle of the music industry. He had built a successful career as a K-pop idol after making his debut as a teenager. He appeared in all the top music programs in Korea and swept the grand prize at multiple award ceremonies. He had been the subject of a few dating rumors, and he achieved huge success in every one of his endeavors, thanks to his remarkable talent.

His punk-like demeanor was a weapon rather than a weakness. His fiery fan base loved his bad-boy image and formed a solid barricade around him that no rumor could break down. His affable personality helped him secure a vast network of connections, and he took advantage of the off-season to expand his horizons and start a business. He was

---

[*] From the Chinese word *chi*, which means "energy." The pronunciation of the Korean word could be described as a mix between "key" and "ghee" but with a short *i* sound.

successful in that, too. He had assets worth multiple millions, luxury homes, and a popularity that never seemed to abate. He had everything one could wish for, a bit like a mighty emperor. His charisma was captivating, and his attitude was always confident and relaxed. He had a large following. Over time, however, his strengths began to fade.

Then, something unexpected happened: He made a series of errors in judgment that caused a number of privacy-related controversies and legal issues that could not be reversed. The rumor mill took these and snowballed, destroying his career. He was exiled from the entertainment industry. Advertisers who had signed exclusive contracts with him began to cancel them, and he was successively dropped from every show he regularly appeared on. Then, the chatter began.

"That's the end of his career."

"I never thought I'd see him go."

Because we knew each other, I couldn't help but feel concerned. I was worried he might be depressed, as some people were saying. It wasn't long before I heard the latest of Alex's news. People said he was hiding in his house, always cooped up inside. I expected him to have given up, lost a lot of weight, and taken steps to retire from the entertainment industry forever. I could not have been more mistaken.

To my surprise, I heard that he was at home studying English. Studying English? Seriously? I suddenly felt like I had been slapped on the back of the head. This guy was something else.

His first thought after the incident had been to leave the country. He had begun preparing to start a new life abroad. It would have been perfectly natural for any entertainer to completely fall apart if their career had ended the way his had. The fact that Alex quickly envisioned a different life was truly remarkable. I was awed by his resilience.

———•

Ben's case was different. Ben had made a successful debut through a televised talent show, but from a producer's perspective, he made the worst first impression among all the candidates. I didn't like his overly laid-back manner. Usually, performers on talent shows don't say much and behave politely to impress the station officials. They're also incredibly nervous because they need to win the audition if they want to get a chance to debut as a singer. As they wait for their turn on stage, some join their hands in prayer and some have such a determined look on their face that it seems like their lives are at stake.

By contrast, Ben exchanged jokes with the writers and seemed to enjoy himself on stage without showing any signs of nervousness. His demeanor was so relaxed that I doubted this was his first public appearance.

What an arrogant person was my first thought, which I quickly realized was another half-baked conclusion on my part. In the beginning, it seemed like he was falling behind.

Surprisingly, he remained collected and continued to perform, and as he approached the second half of the competition, his unflinching, relaxed composure yielded amazing results. Perhaps due to their nervousness, even the best candidates made mistakes they'd never made before or walked off the stage without performing at their best.

On the other hand, Ben kept a cool head until the final round of auditions. Eventually, he rode that momentum to the top and took first place. That's when I realized: He wasn't arrogant, just confident and laid-back. Today, his popularity is such that the public would pay anything to see him.

—•—

People often say that successful people are headstrong. That statement is half right and half wrong. A foolish person who gets swayed by every little thing is not fit to wear a crown. They don't know that when they react to a stimulus, they reveal their vulnerability to their opponents, who are highly likely to use it against them. Being headstrong isn't about being aggressive or overly pushy, but about not being swayed or flustered by the distractions around you.

In that sense, both Alex and Ben are headstrong. In their very different, challenging circumstances, they kept their composure, not letting themselves be agitated or undermined by external stimuli. That serenity is what allowed them to achieve success and popularity.

In reality, people who have a strong personality are usually very gentle, like a Disney character. The main protagonists in Disney movies are assertive and confident in everything they do. They're not constantly on edge or pretending to be strong. They don't need to raise their voices to be recognized, and their effort always yields good results. That was precisely the case with Ben.

You'd be hard-pressed to find a rich person who is not headstrong. The important thing is how you choose to use that unyielding spirit, because that's what will make or break your good fortune.

PEOPLE WHO FAIL CONSISTENTLY HAVE THIS IN COMMON

Busy, modern people are bombarded with the pressure to be positive from the moment they are born: "Always be grateful," "Happiness is within reach," and so on.

Sometimes, that's necessary. But sometimes, those sentiments are a distraction, not a fundamental solution for the difficulties we face. They can often just be sugarcoated pills we're made to swallow to make us believe that things are better than they are. These platitudes don't work at all, especially when it comes to serious matters such as money and success. Why, you ask? Unfortunately, our livelihoods are a life-or-death issue. And you shouldn't sugarcoat something that is that important and valuable.

—•—

Yumi's reality is painful. Fate decided she would be born into a poor family. Her mother has a hearing disability, and her father barely manages to make ends meet by working as a dry cleaner. She doesn't know what the future holds for her, but she still gets good grades despite her difficult circumstances.

She was about to apply for college, but just as she was preparing, she fell in love for the first time and ended up terribly betrayed. Her life fell apart, and she failed to get into the prestigious university she aimed for. She prepared for the exams for another year, going from one prep class to another, but was rejected again. Burying her head in the sand, Yumi started to pretend to be a college student. She lied about her past and education to get hired as a tutor and even married a successful businessman. As she accumulated lie after lie, Yumi's unhappiness snowballed as well.

This is not a real story. It's the plot of the popular K-drama *Anna*. You don't need to see the final episode to guess the catastrophic ending Yumi's lies bring about.

But what should Yumi have done instead? Just keep shouting positive affirmations such as "I'm happy" or "I'm grateful" and ignore her misfortune? Life isn't that easy. Thinking everything is going well doesn't make it any better.

There is really only one answer in a case like this: Be realistic rather than positive.

Being realistic can make your knees shake and your heart race, but it is better to confront reality head-on. Think about it. Wouldn't you rather face your reality, however painful it may be, and break away from it than to disguise your pain with positivity and remain in your abyss forever?

If only Yumi had thought, *My family doesn't have any money, so I need to get my act together,* and had channeled all her energy toward getting into college, she may have encountered genuine luck instead of misfortune.

The same applies when you're upset. There is no virtue or merit in forgiving someone and forgetting when they wronged you. When you have an issue with someone, it's better to confront them and see things through. Contrary to what you might think, that approach will allow you to resolve the situation quickly and move on.

The same is true at work. People feel pressured to put on a positive face while being out in society. That's why you try to be polite and smile even when, deep down, you're having such a hard time you want to turn in your resignation. That type of behavior might earn you a good reputation, but it means you are turning a blind eye to the reality that's causing you to suffer. That is not a winning strategy for dealing with the realities of your life.

———

What you need in the worst situations is not positivity. It is more urgent that you make a conscious effort to become realistic. Rich people are rarely positive, at least not the wealthy people I've met. The simple truth is that the wealthy are unbelievably realistic about money and lead their lives in a characteristically levelheaded way. They thoroughly prioritize themselves, even to the point of selfishness. This doesn't mean you must purposefully keep a pessimistic outlook on everything, but you do need to be honest with yourself and realistic about the situations you are facing.

In that sense, the character of Yumi lacks a sense of reality. That's what made her delude herself into believing she was the daughter of a wealthy family, knowing full well she could never be Anna. Whenever she faced a crisis, Yumi would systematically resort to lying. It was not her intention to lie from the very beginning, but at a certain point, she had gone too far to turn back. Yumi was guilty of living in a fantasy.

"I seek out opportunities now; I no longer believe in luck."

That's a sentence Yumi says in one of the earlier episodes. While it implies that luck has passed her by, she was the first to turn her back on luck. She had plenty of opportunities to turn her life around. She could have gotten a college degree, even if it meant trying a third time. She could have changed her career path and gotten a different job. Her life would have looked completely different had she been able to assess her condition correctly and had enough judgment to solve the challenges she was facing. That is the lesson that the drama *Anna* taught me: Choose to be realistic over being positive, and prioritize myself, not others.

Some people never move past the preparation stage. They never take action. They worry too much and waste their time getting ready to take action. You have to take action to achieve success, but these people remain paralyzed because everything only ever happens inside their heads. They don't want to run out of possibilities.

"It's just that I'm a perfectionist."

"I don't want to show anything before I'm perfectly ready."

There is no luck waiting for you only when you're perfectly ready. One thing is certain, at least if you want to be rich: You have to be a realistic hero, not an optimistic coward.

Daily Habits That Improve Your Financial Luck

Home is where you spend most of your time, making it an excellent base to attract good fortune. Everything in the world has a moving force called energy, and the objects in your home greatly impact your financial fortune.

A typical example are your belongings because they are objects you carry close to your body. This is especially the case for your wallet. Money attracts money. Carrying a 10,000-

won[*] bill rolled up in your wallet will keep wealth from leaking away. Gold cutlery will affect your energy through its color. The color gold has long been associated with wealth, health, and longevity. Simply changing the tools you eat with is enough to attract good fortune.

Such luck-attracting ideas are largely derived from centuries of feng shui. Here are some other things you can do to improve your fortune in your home. Most of them are easy to put into practice once you know them.

1. **Short houseplants are better than tall ones.**
   There is an old saying among adults that plants larger than people suppress human energy. There is a theory that restaurants, cafés, and businesses where many people come and go are good if they have large plants (because they are spaces where many people come and go), but in a family with a small number of people, if there are too-large plants, they will suppress the energy of the householder.

2. **Don't put magnets on the refrigerator.**
   Eating means survival, so in Korea, eating is especially important. Therefore, if there are a lot of unnecessary things attached to the space where food is

[*] Roughly $10 USD.

kept, the aura around the space is not considered clean.

3. **Carry one 10,000-won bill in your wallet.**
In the past, a wallet was considered one's personal storehouse, so there is a belief that carrying actual cash inside it brings good fortune with money. For this reason, in Korea, when giving a wallet as a gift, it is customary to place a little cash inside.

4. **Use gold-colored cutlery.**
The kitchen is a space for handling food, and food is survival, so in the past, the most important thing in the stomach was food. Therefore, it is recommended to use gold or gold-colored tableware in the kitchen, which means money or wealth.

5. **Keep the bathroom door closed.**
Since the toilet has the meaning of washing away bad energy, it is better to close the door so that any unclean energy remaining in the bathroom will not escape to other parts of the living space.

6. **Keep a yellow object in the living room.**
In the Five Energies theory—wood, fire, earth, metal, and water—earth represents stability, balance, and inclusiveness. Since the living room is a place where

the whole family gathers, symbolizing harmony and serving as the center that maintains balance, it is recommended to place yellow items, which represent earth, in this space.

7. **Always keep the front entrance clean.**
The entrance is the first place that receives good energy from outside, so there is a theory that if there are delivery boxes or items piled up, good luck will not be able to enter, but will be blocked.

8. **Sleep with your head next to the window.**
The reason for placing your head near the window is that windows are usually positioned to let in sunlight (in directions other than north). In Korea, it is considered highly inauspicious to sleep with one's head pointing north, because that is believed to be the direction in which the dead are laid to rest. For this reason, Koreans place great importance on having a south-facing home, as the warm sunlight streaming in is seen as a symbol of new beginnings, vitality, and honor.

9. **Put a small plant in the bathroom.**
The bathroom is a place where bad energy stays and then leaves, and a lot of water accumulates, which is said to be a lot of negative energy in Korea. If you

have a lot of yin energy, you need to fill the space with yang energy to achieve harmony. Green plants have yang energy, so it's good to keep them in the bathroom to balance out the yin energy.

10. **Don't keep wet umbrellas inside the house.**
People often leave wet umbrellas at the front door. But doing so brings a stagnant collection of negative energy from the outside that could block the entrance. It is therefore better to store wet umbrellas out of the way to keep the entrance area clean and dry.

The Psychology of
SELF-EXAMINATION

4

The Wealthy Always Find the Answer within Themselves

FOLLOW YOUR NATURE

"I have no idea how to make money."

Scott admitted this with difficulty. He was an entrepreneur who had failed at everything he'd tried since he had retired after a twenty-year-long career as a well-established financial executive. When he was faced with a demotion, he chose to leave the company and go solo.

Because he really liked to exercise, Scott decided to develop a health-care app. However, to develop it, he had to invest a large portion of the money he had carefully saved during his two-decade career. The app never made a profit. Scott gave up on the application and instead tried to run a fitness center, but that didn't work out either. He had poured all his money, including his retirement savings, into his new endeavors. Alas, he was left with considerable losses after failing two times in a row. The financial challenges affected his family life as well.

"You must familiarize yourself with your Energy first," I said to him.

"Sorry? What do you mean?" Scott asked, suddenly sitting up straight.

"Every person has their own Energy. That knowledge alone will help you figure out how to make money. You have heard of the concept of 'personal color,' right? Every individual has different colors and clothing styles they look best in depending on their unique physical attributes like skin tone and body type. That's because we all have a unique physical palette. Nowadays, you can easily find experts who offer consulting services and help you find your personal color. Such services have become very trendy because wearing clothes or makeup that fit your personal color is a simple yet effective way to improve your appearance.

"You can think of the Energy I mentioned as something very similar to the idea of a personal color. You can find out what your personal Energy is, just like you can identify your personal color. If you don't know what it is already, you need to figure it out."

Most of the wealthy people I know are interested in the science of Myeongli. They go to great lengths to find good teachers and learn more. Watching them made me wonder why they were working so tirelessly to discover more about their fortune when these people already had so much.

Thinking about it now, I think I understand the reason. Studying Myeongli allows you to decipher your own fortune. The wealthy who studied it so diligently were trying to analyze and use their personal energy to seize even more luck even more quickly. That's the reason I told Scott he had to learn about his own energy. Many rich people already put that knowledge into practice in their lives.

I gave Scott another piece of information: "People who are good at making money and growing it have a deep knowledge of themselves and at least a basic understanding of Oh-haeng[*] (the Five Energies theory). They know what they can and cannot do and are good at applying that knowledge in their daily lives. That's how they become even wealthier."

"Oh-haeng, the Five Energies?" he asked me.

"Yes, simply put, the Five Energies that make up the world. It's nothing complicated. On the contrary, it's something that's as natural as the flow of the seasons: Wood (木), Fire (火), Earth (土), Metal (金), and Water (水). These five types of

---

[*] Oh (five) haeng (movement, flow, generally translated into "energy" in Korean).

energy constitute the foundation of both nature and humanity. Everything moves in cycles, just like the moon rises as the sun sets, and the moon wanes after reaching the full stage. Humans are part of nature, so we follow that cycle, too. And so does luck."

"You mean *everything* goes in circles?"

"Yes. Here is an example. We use wood for fire. After it's burnt, the leftover ashes return to earth. As the earth solidifies, it turns into rocks or metal. Water flows through these rocks or hard metal, seeping through the earth and feeding the trees. Every element comes and goes in circles, helping the others. Once you know where you are situated in that cycle of energy, or what energy you currently possess, you will see what's going to bring you money."

"I see. So if I figure out what my personal energy is, that's going to teach me how to live within that cycle?"

"That's right. Try to picture nature. Trees sink their roots deep into the earth and soar toward the sky. That's why people with wood energy tend to have high ideals and enjoy being creative, just like how trees bear fruits on their branches. People who have fire energy are consistent with the image you have of fire. They're passionate people who are all about action, and they value honor. They don't mind public attention either. That's why you'll find a lot of them are particularly talented in the arts or sports. The earth is the soil that makes up the basis of life. It stretches wide, it is calm, and it embraces everything around it, which is why people with earth energy are a good fit for tasks that require patience. What do you think? You get the idea, right? Can you guess what metal does?"

"Hmm. Well, metal feels cold and hard. It's also something you refine with fire . . . ?"

"Precisely. People with a strong metal energy are rational and realistic, like a well-polished blade or gem. They are level-headed people who are thorough and good with detailed, delicate tasks. Lastly, water. It flows downward, taking everything in and mixing it all together. So people with water energy learn a lot and continuously challenge themselves because they're good at absorbing external elements. They excel at intellectual tasks."

I told him the story of someone I knew as an example.

———

Alice was a passionate person who also had a fantastic personality. Outgoing and cheerful, she knew how to run the show and was quick to set the mood in any environment. On top of that, she was a "people person," a blast to be around.

"I've liked being the center of attention ever since I was a child. I was never the first to suggest a trip to karaoke, but once I got a hold of the microphone, you couldn't take it away from me. I think I already knew at the time that I was going to appear on TV."

Her smiling eyes showed confidence as she stared into the

camera. She stood out from the very beginning. Objectively speaking, she wasn't "beauty pageant" beautiful, but she captivated the world of entertainment from the start with her bubbly personality, and she was not afraid to take the stage in front of a large audience. She attracted everyone's attention early on by becoming the news anchor for the station. Despite such a successful debut, Alice increasingly felt out of place.

As the main news anchor, her job required her to wear a professional suit with a formal hairstyle and to deliver speeches in the same dull tone. She smiled most gracefully in front of the camera, but somehow, the role didn't fit her. Hosting a cultural program didn't suit her personality. She felt like she was in somebody else's clothes. She wasn't the only one who noticed it; viewers wrote in with comments like, "She doesn't look comfortable," or "I couldn't focus on the show."

Alice made up her mind to take action. As per her usual fiery self, she didn't hesitate. She turned in her resignation, not waiting to end the situation that she knew was not right for her.

"I don't want to leave broadcasting for good. What should I do?"

She wanted to connect with the audience as she had when she was an up-and-comer. A year and a half after resigning as a news host, she resurfaced as the host of a very different type of show: home shopping. It turned out to be an excellent choice. Unlike on the news, Alice was able to have fun, giving free rein to her happy, bubbly personality.

She had made the right bet. It didn't matter if she spewed food out of her mouth, bursting with laughter during a food segment, or messed up her hair during a hair roller demonstration gone wrong. She handled every unexpected situation with humor and flair. In fact, her quirkiness and spontaneity made viewers like and trust her even more, contributing to high ratings and sales.

She had soon captivated the audience, considered such a treasure in the home shopping industry that she even earned the nickname "The Home Shopping Lady Who Can Sell Out Anything." Her salary climbed rapidly, and rumors started circulating that she had moved into an apartment in a building only the wealthiest could afford to buy.

The power of energy was the key reason why Alice was able to reach hundreds of millions of viewers annually and earn millions per hour in revenue. She sold out whatever products she featured on every single show. She was incredibly lucky to have found a job that matched her energy so quickly after taking the risk to resign from a job that did not fit her.

In terms of Oh-haeng, Alice has fire energy. She is meant to shine like the sun. As an anchor, having a script to follow worked against her energy; it must have been hard to bend to such constraints. In the end, Alice found a new career path that allowed her to use her energy in a way that suited her and yielded great results. Even now, Alice probably doesn't know what her Oh-haeng is. However, she must be aware that it was her inherent nature, pushing her to shine like the sun and radiate energy, that was at the root of her immense fortune.

———

If a person doesn't know the first thing about Oh-haeng, is there a way they can learn about their energy type? If you have figured out which energy you possess, whether the discovery was on your own or with help, that alone makes you lucky. Most people go about their lives ignoring this crucial information about themselves.

One way to get a clue to your energy is to look at your lineage. Your family and the environment you were born and grew up in allows you to draw a rough picture. You may have noticed, but artists often come from a family of artists, and the same goes for athletes.

You may also be familiar with sayings such as "You can't fool blood," or "They probably get that from me," or "It runs in the family." That can only mean one of two things: Either you have inherited a family trait or you have been frequently exposed to that particular kind of energy.

The first ones to take notice of a child's energy are usually the parents. A fully supportive family, in addition to the person's own effort, can lead to the development of a genius. Unfortunately, few are lucky enough to have all three: inherent energy, supportive parents, and one's own efforts.

You can also twist this theory in a cynical way, arguing that luck from birth really only favors those who are born to wealthy parents.

The truth is, no matter how much money you have, you are more likely to fail if you choose the wrong path because you have no knowledge of your inherent energy.

———

Bill was born into a wealthy family of doctors. The youngest of his siblings, from the beginning, Bill was set on an elite track. His father was an orthopedic surgeon at a renowned university hospital, and his eldest brother was following in his footsteps.

But that's not what Bill was interested in. He had been an accomplished singer since he was a young child. He was also an excellent guitar player—so good, in fact, that it was difficult to believe his skills were self-taught. He must have inherited his musical talent from his maternal grandfather.

Passionate about music, Bill started dreaming of a career in the entertainment industry. He even auditioned for a top entertainment agency when he was in high school and made it through the first round of auditions. He kept it a secret from his family, but his parents found out about it as Bill was about to take part in the second audition. A singer in a family of doctors? The entire family was enraged.

Faced with such fierce opposition, Bill had to make a choice: go to medical school as his parents wanted, or follow his dream to become a singer. It was a difficult decision. Bill had never disobeyed his parents, and his top grades reflected the money his parents poured into his education. In the end, he felt he had to follow his parents' wishes and became a dentist.

When he reached his mid-thirties, however, Bill suddenly started to feel depressed for no apparent reason. He had a stable life with a nice family—what could possibly be missing? One day, Bill took out his old guitar, wiped off the thick layer of dust that had accumulated on it, and tuned the strings.

As he began to play, just like when he was in high school, he was surprised to discover his hands remembered the chords. Bill felt exhilarated. It was like someone had turned on a bright light in his heart. Taken aback, he resolved never to lose that feeling again.

Bill never became a famous singer. He continues to work as a doctor, but he relieves his regret through song.

———•———

People who have correctly identified their energy are more likely to reach the highest peaks of success. By contrast, those who ignore their energy are more likely to regret the choices they have made.

One piece of advice I often give my clients is this: "Live in accordance with your nature." Nature, by definition, designates the traits you are born with. If you want things to work out for you, you have to live in harmony with your inherent character. Would you rather force yourself to adapt to every situation as it arises, not knowing what your personal energy is? Or would you rather be mindful of your energy and choose the path that will help you make the best use of it? Your answer to these questions can change the pace of your life. That's how crucial finding your energy is.

That's the reason why successful people study Myeongli so assiduously. Once you have identified what energy you were born with, you will be better able to discern your strengths and weaknesses and know who to avoid and whose company you must seek out. Although the answers you find may not be as straightforward as the result of a math equation, you will still be able to work out a general direction.

Correctly discerning your inherent temperament is enough to help improve your luck. It is within your power to realize your energy and make good decisions based on that knowledge. Not taking the time to be aware of it could mean you miss out on important opportunities and paths to success.

THE "FORTUNE" OF "MISFORTUNE"

Luck is closely tied to your inherent character and how you employ it. What matters most is that you approach the events of your life while making the most of your inherent character. I have discovered a few common threads in the stories people confide in me. First of all, so many people find themselves in such confusing and difficult situations that they are not prepared for. Secondly, incredibly unlikely, unexpected, and upsetting events happen much more often and to many more people than you would expect. What always astonishes me are the successful people I meet who nonetheless always manage to find solutions that benefit them, even in the most unimaginable and absurd circumstances.

———•———

This is the story of an entrepreneur who ran a bubble tea business. They were so successful that, at some point, they had more than a thousand shops across South Korea. The company just kept growing bigger and bigger every day. The company actually had two founders, Arthur and Brian. Strictly speaking, it was Arthur who started the company when he opened a small bubble tea shop in a university town. Although he had joined Arthur later, it was Brian who grew the business to its current size.

Their story had begun years before, when one day a random young man turned up at Arthur's shop, asking him to teach him about the business.

"I'd like to learn from you."

"Excuse me?"

"I want to grow this business. I know I can do it."

Arthur had been just about to hire a part-timer, as he had been struggling to run the shop on his own. Although Arthur was somewhat bewildered by Brian's bold confidence, he taught him the ropes.

From that moment on, the small bubble tea shop started raking in money. Brian was exceptionally bright. He understood customers' needs and desires as if he had been in the business for decades. He categorically stated that college students would never spend money at their shop if the products were expensive. Brian convinced Arthur that they needed to start selling bubble tea for under 2,000 won.[*] Flavorful drinks and shockingly low prices turned out to be a winning combination. Word spread quickly about the small bubble tea shop that offered tasty drinks at affordable prices.

[*] Less than $1.50 USD.

Without even taking a breather, Brian scanned the neighboring areas, on the hunt for the best location to open their second shop. College towns were overflowing with small cafés. He first targeted areas highly frequented by pedestrians, where he approached small café owners and convinced them they could easily transition to a bubble tea shop with a little bit of remodeling. He also added that it was much more strategic to sell trendy new drinks and offer different products instead of being one of the many small fish in an ocean of coffee shops.

Brian gradually recruited more and more franchisees to join their business network. The burgeoning new shop fronts intrigued passersby, making them wonder, *What kind of shop is that?* or noting, "I'm spotting more and more of those." Some even pondered joining the franchise themselves.

In the initial stages, Brian focused on neighborhoods near colleges. Then, he wanted to expand to larger commercial areas that had more foot traffic and customers with more spending power. *Where is the first place I would go if I were thinking of starting a business?* he wondered.

He had an epiphany. He went to a start-up fair, where he met with small café owners with little capital and convinced them of the high profitability of the bubble tea business.

"There are too many cafés everywhere. A bubble tea shop is a much better choice."

Joining their bubble tea business required considerably

less initial investment than a regular café franchise. On top of that, Brian promised to find prime real estate for them in a university town, which made his proposal very tempting indeed. The bubble tea brand grew rapidly, securing the highest number of franchisees in the shortest time frame. In addition, they managed to establish themselves as the original premium bubble tea brand.

That wasn't all. In addition to the regular profits accrued from royalties, every franchise generated considerable one-time revenue from the interior design and setup fees. Brian had created a sustainable revenue scheme and a solid structure for the company, putting the business on a steady growth path.

At first glance, Brian seems like a person who has always been wealthy and successful. In reality, he was born into a terribly poor family. He wasn't even able to finish school properly, which meant he never had the opportunity to get any formal education or training about business or management. The only thing he had going for himself was his "sense of observation."

Brian's parents were obsessed with horse racing.

Instead of going to school, Brian worked at a private race-track, handing out bottles of Bacchus[*] to customers. He earned pocket money by running errands for the adults who came to take part in illegal gambling. Catering to a cash-

---

[*] A Korean energy drink.

crazed crowd sharpened his insight and taught him how to "read" people—what they liked and what they disliked. That's how he learned the ins and outs of business.

You could say he'd had a miserable childhood. Understandably, he could have gone down the wrong path. Instead, he found a way out of poverty and the lack of opportunity.

Unfortunately, people like Brian are rare. Most people look for an answer in the lives of other people who have nothing to do with them, not within their own. It is unwise to mistake your hobby for an escape; often, a hobby is just a hobby. In Korea, many people who leave their corporate jobs decide to start a fried chicken restaurant business. Why would they expect to succeed when they don't know the first thing about the restaurant business? Wouldn't it make more sense for them to do something that's related to their previous occupation?

Let's say you want to change jobs after working as a hairdresser for years. It is very likely that you can make money if you do something in the same field, like developing new hair-related equipment or dyes. But if you've worked your whole life as a hairdresser and suddenly start a bakery, just because you've "always liked baking," the result is likely to be a disaster and failure, not profit and success.

Everybody has an area of focus, no matter how menial it might seem. If you have been doing something consistently for at least the past three years, it means that's the direction your fortune is going toward, for better or for worse. So do your best to stay focused on what you're currently doing, and even if you need to look for a different answer, stay within those boundaries.

You can take simple steps right away. Keep your mind focused. Whatever mood they might be in, happy or sad, wise people always forge their own luck within the path and area that they find themselves in at the moment. Working with what is in front of you, in fact, is also the fastest way to wealth.

LUCK NEEDS PRIORITIES

As you age, your brain function is thought to decline and your memory and sense of judgment get worse. In reality, the elderly are not the only ones who are affected by this issue. Young people can also experience lapses in judgment when they go through a traumatic event or are faced with an overwhelming challenge, as if their brain had stopped working.

Issues related to relationships, school, jobs, etc. are relatively minor. You can always meet someone else, retake a test, or apply to a different company. However, losing all of your money or falling from the top of your game is a different story. The consequences of losing your money or your status are devastating. When lost, these things take a long time to recover.

In your own life, when you encounter an issue that you

feel could be so devastating that you can't think straight, what is the first thing you should do? Some people worry that there are things they can't handle, even more so if life throws them multiple crises simultaneously. Even the most sensible of us would be perturbed in situations like that.

In my work, I have witnessed many people freeze when they found themselves in a vulnerable position, seemingly unable to think. Fortunately, I have learned that there is almost always a way to solve these problems if you keep your wits about you. On the other hand, I have also seen people, whose brains seem to completely shut down from shock, make hurried choices under pressure and go down a path they will never be able to come back from.

Jesse is a trainer at a gym run by a close friend of his. He had great ambitions. He wanted to create a health food brand under his name, based on his expertise in nutrition and his experience as a coach.

However, putting his plan into action was not so easy. The gym had been losing members every month. Jesse was worried. He wasn't sure he would be able to keep his job at the gym, let alone start a business.

In addition, his girlfriend wanted them to get married, but with what money? He didn't even have enough to buy a studio apartment. His life was a mess. He couldn't figure out why he was having so much trouble when he was doing his absolute best.

"I have no idea where I went wrong."

"You mean the cause of your current problems?"

"Yes. I can't think. It's a disaster. I can't quit my job because I have bills to pay. At the same time, I feel uncomfortable asking my friend for my paycheck when we are continuously losing members. Same with marriage. I do love my girlfriend, but we can't afford to live together right now. I feel like I'm just going to get old without ever being able to start a business."

Listening to this, I realized Jesse's problems were already as good as solved. He had just temporarily gotten lost in a sudden storm. It was clear he already had a solution; he just hadn't realized it yet. I gave him a little hint.

"Just think: What's the single most important thing to you?"

First, Jesse looked puzzled. Suddenly, the expression on his face changed.

A few months later, I heard back from Jesse. He called to tell me the good news. I could hear him beaming through the phone.

"Ms. Yoo, I can see things more clearly now. You told me to focus on one thing and one thing only. Looking back, that was the key to everything. You were right. There was only one problem I needed to solve. I thought I would never be able to get myself out of this mess, but everything changed, just like magic!"

Jesse told me what had happened. After our meeting, he had gone home, sat down at his desk, and made a list of everything he had to do. He thought, *What's the one thing that matters most to me right now?* He immediately knew the answer. For him, it was work. He knew that resolving his work issues would make everything else easier. He understood what he had to do next and immediately sprang into action. He started applying to jobs at other gyms first thing the next morning.

He happened to meet the owner at the first gym he wanted to apply to as the owner was getting ready to open for business. The gym was a long-established fitness center located inside a luxury hotel. If Jesse had left his résumé with a random employee, it could have ended up in the trash. Thanking his lucky stars, Jesse greeted the owner with a bright smile and handed him his résumé. He was hired shortly afterward. Was it fate?

Jesse's luck didn't end there. It kept on going, like falling domino pieces. He worked harder than anybody at his new workplace. He cared for each of his clients the best he could, which attracted more members, which in turn led to higher pay. What's more, he was able to make connections with VIP members because the owner had put him in charge of an expensive diet and fitness management program reserved for elite members.

Soon, his relationship problems resolved themselves, too. He left his previous gym as membership declined and tensions rose. Instead of resentment, his friend felt gratitude toward him for decreasing his payroll at a difficult time, and the two became closer. Little by little, Jesse got recognition at his new workplace, was able to save more money, and finally married his girlfriend. Moreover, he started discussing how to invest in the health food industry, thanks to a client of his who had been impressed by his work and wanted to help him out.

Jesse had already had the answer. The competing problems and pressures of daily life had caused him to lose sight of what was truly urgent.

Monthly credit card fees, his relationships with the people around him, marriage with his girlfriend, etc.—Jesse had not known what to prioritize. All the other issues could work themselves out one by one once he resolved the most important one: his work life. Jesse's indecision was the main obstacle preventing him from resolving his problems efficiently.

There is an order of priority in everything, including in one's lifelong luck. There are issues that you must settle immediately, issues that you must resolve first in order to move on to the next stage. Sometimes, it might feel like your whole life is a mess of a million troubles, but once you take a closer look, there is often only one problem you need to solve.

Even when it seems like you're holding a tangled ball of yarn with no beginning or end, you will eventually be able to work everything out once you find the knot. In life, straightening out your order of priorities can make a big difference.

PUT YOUR LIFE ON THE CHOPPING BLOCK, AND START HACKING AWAY

But how do you set the order of priority?

It is easy to confuse what's important with what's urgent. Before anything else, you must first break down your life and look at it carefully. That will help you dissolve bad luck and start fresh. I didn't tell Jesse the answer. I just advised him to figure out "the single most important thing" to him and taught him a few ways to look at life from different angles.

"You need to do some knifework."

"What? Knifework?!"

"Yes. You need to put your life on a table and dissect it."

Jesse confessed he had never faced his problems, analyzed them, and prioritized what needed to be fixed first. When faced with the harsh realities of life, he only tried to run away from them, never confronting them head-on. No wonder he could never make any money, when all he was doing was looking for shortcuts. To get a hold of good fortune is never as easy as people think. But now, Jesse has learned how to put his life on a chopping block and examine it in detail.

The wealthy are no different. You wouldn't believe the methods they use to set their priorities. There was a wealthy gentleman who had earned a fortune thanks to his exceptional skill in recognizing valuable land before it rose in price. Even the questions he asked me were out of the ordinary. When he came to ask me for some investing advice, he brought a map with him on which he had marked all the land he owned across the country. He said he wasn't curious about anything other than land. He focused on one goal and one goal only. In my experience, people who know exactly what they want usually reach their objective without too much trouble.

By contrast, there are people who haven't got a clue how to prioritize—or even worse, who have never thought about prioritizing at all. I can just tell by the questions they ask me. Their questions are so vague and abstract, it's hard to grasp what it is they even want to know. They bring up problems from the past, global issues that aren't pertinent to their immediate lives, and irrelevant people. Their questions make it clear that they are chasing clouds and don't have the faintest idea what they should prioritize. The contrast between these two groups of people could not be more striking.

Observing successful people has given me the impression that they truly know their priorities. Successful people even seem to know what to prioritize when and how to direct their luck.

If you think about it, the same logic applies to the top and bottom students in a class. Even if they both take the same test, the student who understands precisely the intention behind the questions, and the student who fails to grasp the point are not going to get the same outcome. Obviously. The top student studied five hours a day on average, and the bottom student spent twice that time. They both studied hard, but they got different results. The top student studied sample questions from previous tests, based on what the teacher had emphasized during class. The bottom one heard the exam questions would be based on the textbook. He opened his book to page 1, grabbed his highlighters, and began to learn everything by heart, filling the pages with all the colors of the rainbow. I don't need to tell you that this student is headed for complete failure.

This is why it is so important to get your priorities straight. The bottom-ranked student might have had a different fate if he'd had a remarkable private tutor who told him what to prioritize for the test. However, you can't always rely on somebody else to determine your priorities for you. You must figure that out by yourself.

———•———

Ultimately, nobody can live your life for you. There is no one exact equation, as in mathematics, that enables any of us to correctly diagnose and prescribe the right solutions and priorities in the life of another person.

There is a saying: "Even the most competent doctor can't operate on their own family member." Their personal feelings would get in the way. And even I can't keep my personal thoughts from getting in the way when reading the fortune of a friend.

That's why nobody but you should define your own order of priorities. There is a very simple way to go about it: Tackle the thing that makes you feel the weakest first. You should be prepared to tackle all of your problems one after the other. Problems that you want to ignore seldom go away easily.

The person who created the problem should be the one to solve it. Unfortunately, however, you may often find yourself in situations where you have to solve a problem you had nothing to do with. It's unfair, but that won't make the problem disappear. If it's something you need to resolve anyway, start breaking it down instead of wasting time blaming others or the world.

Once you have decided what your number one priority is, just put it on the table and start "hacking away" at it. If getting out of debt is your most important priority, you must first figure out how you got into debt, then determine the exact amount of money you need to pay off. Next, you need to decide how you are going to generate income, calculate the probabilities of success, and when you can expect to have paid off the debt in full. Laying out the problem in front of you and dissecting it can give you very clear insight into your life.

As you begin hacking away, you will notice that the situation becomes less fraught and less complicated. Once your number one priority, the problem you are focused on solving, has your full attention, your fortune will shift and money and luck will follow like a school of fish.

DON'T SET THE OUTCOME IN STONE

Life is a succession of tests.

From elementary school to high school, you take exams every semester to prepare for graduation. And it doesn't stop when you get into college. You take tests to prove your worth as a job seeker and an official member of society after you get your first job.

And still, there are more tests to come, from licensing exams to promotion tests. In short, you are trapped in a series of tests for much of your life. Why do people put themselves through so much trouble? College? A job? A promotion? Self-realization? All are correct answers.

Passing tests turns into symbolic milestones as you try to climb the ladder of success. People who pass particularly difficult tests become figures of success and luck for the rest of us. But behind each of these success stories is a more difficult reality about luck we must reckon with. What you see isn't everything, and another's success following a certain path won't necessarily predict your own future. What is important to you and what society decrees as important may not coincide. There are a lot of examples that teach us this lesson, especially in exams, where results can have a distinct and lasting impact.

—•—

"I'm moving to Noryangjin* soon."

I had a friend, Charlotte, who was studying for the civil service exam. Working for the government was considered one of the most respected professions at the time. I was surprised by Charlotte's decision to jump into such an unfamiliar territory that no one else among our college friends was interested in. Deep down, however, I felt I could at least understand a small part of her motivation. Charlotte was an only child, and her parents had high expectations for her; their goal for her life was to secure a stable living. So Charlotte took a year off to dedicate herself entirely to preparing for the exam.

Nonetheless, Charlotte returned to school after only a year.

---

* An area in the southwest of Seoul populated with cram schools and dorm-like facilities for the students who attend them. The intense studying atmosphere in Noryangjin is supposed to help wannabe civil servants prepare for public service exams.

With a deep sigh, she explained that she had failed the exam even though she had studied assiduously.

Not long after, she took a leave of absence again and went back to Noryangjin. Despite all of her efforts, she failed a second time.

Charlotte couldn't give up. She kept trying.

About a year after graduation, I heard the good news: She had finally been accepted into the civil service. When we saw each other again, Charlotte was beaming.

"You finally made it!"

"Yes! I'll work for the government until my dying day. I'll keep climbing the ladder."

I was so proud of her for persevering and succeeding despite the fierce competition. Our fellow classmates congratulated her, wishing her good luck. She was still a young woman in her twenties, but her future was assured. We each set off on our respective paths, me to a broadcasting station as a producer, she to a district office as a civil servant.

Not a year had passed before I heard of Charlotte's news. I couldn't believe it: She had quit her job in government that she had worked so hard to get. I was curious what had happened.

At first, the joy of getting her dream job had kept her going. But as the excitement abated, Charlotte found it increasingly difficult to adjust to the hierarchical and conservative organizational culture. On days when they were flooded with complaints, she had to forget about going home for the night. Getting into arguments with the residents about petty grievances over mosquitoes and noise was another source of stress. Charlotte was too free-spirited and sensitive. Work had consumed her inner peace bit by bit. She tried her best to stick it out, but she gave up after a year.

"Getting accepted was not the end. The day-to-day reality was nothing like I expected," she said.

THE LUCKY CHEST OR THE LUCKY CHARM BOX

Luck is like a rugby ball: It's impossible to guess where it might be headed next and when. Something that had seemed like good luck at one moment can turn out to be bad luck at another. Or you may realize that something you had considered bad luck at the time was actually good luck. Money is the same. The fact that you have some in your hand right now doesn't mean it will stay there, or that any money you don't have will become someone else's. The same logic applies to luck, too.

There was once a poor old man. One night, his great-grandmother appeared in his dream and told him the winning numbers for the lottery. The old man was so happy, he went around town telling everybody that he had won the lottery. The night he retrieved the money, he got robbed. The robber took his prize money, but also the few other possessions he had. The old man was devastated. He had gone bankrupt as quickly as he had gotten rich. Now, do you think winning the lottery was a good thing for him or a bad thing?

Of course, a windfall can be considered good luck. How long that luck lasts, however, is a different matter. Success and failure may depend on luck, but anything that happens afterward is entirely up to you. There is no denying that attracting good luck is essential. But that's not enough. Keeping that luck and making it last is of equal importance.

You would do better to adopt a long-term perspective when it comes to fate. Always keep an even temperament, and don't let your impulses guide you. The money that's in your hands today is not going to stay there forever, just like passing a test is not a guarantee for lifelong success. Opulence has no value if the container that holds it is unfit to retain a fortune of that magnitude.

Which are you going to use to house your luck, a large chest or a small box? What matters more than immediate luck is your ability to handle it.

THE COMMANDER SENT FROM HEAVEN

There are as many rich people in the entertainment industry as there are in the business world. Popularity translates into commercial value, which, in the market economy, means money. Celebrities can get paid anything from a few thousand dollars to a few million for appearing in a commercial.

Becoming a star is one of the fastest and surest ways to climb the social ladder. Once your face becomes known to the public or a work you starred in becomes a big hit, your price tag goes through the roof. That's why so many find it hard to not get their hopes up, even if luck is invisible. They expectantly wait for the opportunity that will turn them into a star overnight, for the life of a celebrity who gets paid millions per day.

There is no free lunch in the world, and the world of luck is no exception. The spotlight also has a price tag. The more love and attention you get, the more gossip and noise you will attract. However, it's something that comes with the job when your livelihood depends on popularity and fame. Perhaps freedom and dignity are the price you pay in exchange for riches and social status.

———•———

One day, I experienced a moment of déjà vu as I switched the TV channel.

"This is your first public appearance in ten years. Aren't you scared?" a journalist asked.

"If you go out on a rainy day, you should expect at least your collar to get wet, even if you have an umbrella."

On the TV screen, an A-list actor who had left the entertainment business when they got married was holding a press conference to officially announce their return to the entertainment industry. The actor was radiating an aura that made it hard to believe they had been gone for ten years. This was no ordinary interview. It was the kind of event that sent waves through the national culture. Blunt questions were being thrown around by the press, and there was a constant burst of camera flashes.

Contrary to the enthusiastic response from the media, the public was divided about the actor suddenly coming out of retirement after disappearing from the spotlight at the height of their career. One half felt betrayed that the actor had gone back on their word, and the other half welcomed them back with open arms.

In the middle of all this tumult, the actor sat perfectly at ease, without the slightest sign of disquiet. Their posture was upright and assured, and their gaze was firm and direct. It was as if they had prepared for this moment and rehearsed everything in their head. What was their secret?

What they had said a few moments earlier seemed to imply that they were ready to face the gossip, criticism, and hateful comments. This self-assurance was the basis for their confident attitude in front of a sea of cameras.

———

People who excel in their field, like this actor, have a different perspective on everything. Little criticisms and idle gossip are a small price to pay for their success.

A good example of grace under pressure is Shilla Hotels President Lee Boojin, the eighth-richest entrepreneur in Korea. Several years ago, a taxi driver in his eighties crashed into the revolving door of the Shilla Hotel in Jangchung-dong, Seoul. Hotel personnel were injured, and the revolving door was smashed to pieces. If Shilla Hotels had sought compensation, the cab driver would have faced more than three hundred thousand dollars in damages. After receiving a briefing on the incident, President Lee ordered a visit to the taxi driver's home to assess the situation. It turned out that, on top of being in poor health himself, the aged taxi driver was looking after his wife, who had been hospitalized after a stroke. Lee concluded the case by not only exonerating the driver of the damages caused to the hotel, but also by covering the elderly couple's hospital fees. The Korean society was deeply touched by the story when it spread through the media. Lee's ability to overlook the smaller things for the benefit of what truly mattered had generated more good publicity than money could buy.

Rain, the global K-pop star, is another example. The singer had recently gained an unusual amount of attention for a song he had released years ago. Unfortunately, it wasn't positive attention. The younger generation had been making a mockery of the badly-aged lyrics and Rain's performance style at the time, which had long since gone out of fashion. Instead of getting upset, Rain showed the opposite reaction of what one would expect in such a case: He enjoyed people's reactions.

In the end, his acceptance of the criticism, his enjoyment of it, reversed public opinion about him. Those who had once made fun of him and his work came to like and admire him. The public's sentiment toward Rain had changed so strongly that he rose to stardom all over again.

What if Rain had fixated on immediate gain or his short-term public image? Would he have managed to attract such favorable opinion from the public if he had shown his displeasure at the youngsters, accusing them of libel and slander? Rain was able to convert haters into admirers because he displayed the energy of a "commander sent from heaven" who turns any situation that he's given in his favor.

———•———

Sun Tzu, the author of *The Art of War*,[*] differentiated generals into three different types. The first is the "courageous leader"; they use their exceptional skills to take the lead in problem-solving. "Strategic leaders" have brilliant tactics, and "moral leaders" draw courageous leaders and strategic leaders under their command with their virtuous behavior.

A courageous leader cannot defeat a strategic leader, nor can a strategic leader defeat a moral leader. But no matter how

---

[*] An ancient Chinese military treatise from the late Spring and Autumn period (c. 770–c. 481 B.C.E.). It is composed of thirteen chapters, each of which deals with a different set of skills or art related to warfare and how it applies to military strategy and tactics.

hard they try, all three together would never be able to measure up to the last category of leader, the "leader sent from heaven."

The actor who announced their return through a press conference took command over their own fortune and made a spectacular comeback in a show that garnered top ratings. Their self-assurance allowed them not to get caught up in the small things and to adopt a broader perspective, bringing them an even bigger success than before.

People who are destined for success appraise things in a completely different way. They tolerate small losses and take home even bigger winnings. By contrast, people who seem to consistently run into trouble lose big and win small. They assign too much importance to minor luck and let the kind of luck that is crucial to them slip away. That's why you should neither dwell on the minutiae or be wasteful with luck.

Everybody comes across good luck, but it is up to each individual to decide how big or small it is going to be.

FIND YOUR WAY IN THREE SECONDS WITH YOUR FINGERTIPS

What are two unavoidable aspects of human existence that persist throughout life? The first is failure, and the second is taxes. Not even a head of state can do anything about taxes, but sometimes, it's possible to find a way to escape failure or at least use it as a way to evolve and move forward.

This is something a mentor taught me a long time ago, but I had completely forgotten about it until recently. Then I started reading fortunes, and a particular moment kept coming back to me, reminding me of a lecture where my mentor revealed one of life's secrets to me: "To all the people who are struggling because they feel stuck, I would like to say, 'This is how you move forward,' and tell them that taking things one small step at a time is good enough."

Spring had come early that year. A professor I have always liked and admired told me over a meal:

"People are constantly tormented by the impression they're being idle although they're busy all the time. That is especially true for people who are desperate for money and success. The truth is, no one is ever not doing anything. A stay-at-home spouse takes care of the house, a student attends classes, and an employee performs their tasks. When you get the feeling that you're the only one lagging behind and can't keep up, not only does it make you impatient, but it also obscures your entire worldview. You can never succeed with a mindset like that."

"What do you mean, professor?"

"Think about it. Viewing yourself as idle makes you feel inadequate. That sort of defeatist thinking instills the belief that the successful are a category of people you can never be a part of. When you think like this, success seems increasingly elusive, and all that's left in your memory is what feels like a series of failures. Success eventually becomes something that seems completely separate from you. With more memories of failure and fewer of success, it becomes more difficult to see and recognize your successes. Success moves out of sight, and thus out of mind."

The professor had a point. If you lowered your psychological resistance toward failure, you could acquire a better sense about success. By refraining from naming all the things you are actually doing as idleness and failure, you can see all the things you are actually doing as small successes. This creates a memory bank of successes. By accumulating more and more experience of success, you will reduce the probability of failure, which means you are that much closer to achieving wealth.

I remember reading about a study that supported this argument. A team of researchers discovered that humans' tendency to hold on to bad memories longer is directly related to our deep survival instinct. Imagine seeing a small ball of fur in the bushes and taking a little too long to realize it wasn't a rabbit or a deer, but a lion's tail. After our ancestors narrowly escaped death from that lion, the traumatic memory of fear had been etched into their brains, reminding them to always avoid brown patches of fur in the future. Each traumatic experience adds another bad memory to our database. The researchers have hypothesized that these memories are passed down to our descendants so they can survive, too.

The brain converts life-threatening experiences into long-term memories so we don't repeat them. Similarly, your memory about a particular event is going to last longer if you perceive an experience of failure as a threat. Your memory is then going to save primarily experiences of failure, even if they don't actually coincide with the reality of the event. When your library of memories is always stocked with books of failures, that is only going to push success away from you. Our human abilities are not strong enough to allow us to grasp reality as it is. What ends up blocking our path to success, then, are incomplete memories of failure.

"What do you do, then, professor? What do you do when you're stagnating sometimes and feel that you're not getting anywhere. What's your solution?"

"You change your approach to success. You take a good look at it with your own eyes."

"With my eyes?"

———

You can't avoid paying taxes, even if you're the head of the government, that much is certain. However, there are ways to reduce the number of failures by looking at them in a different way. Based on what my professor said, it was an attainable

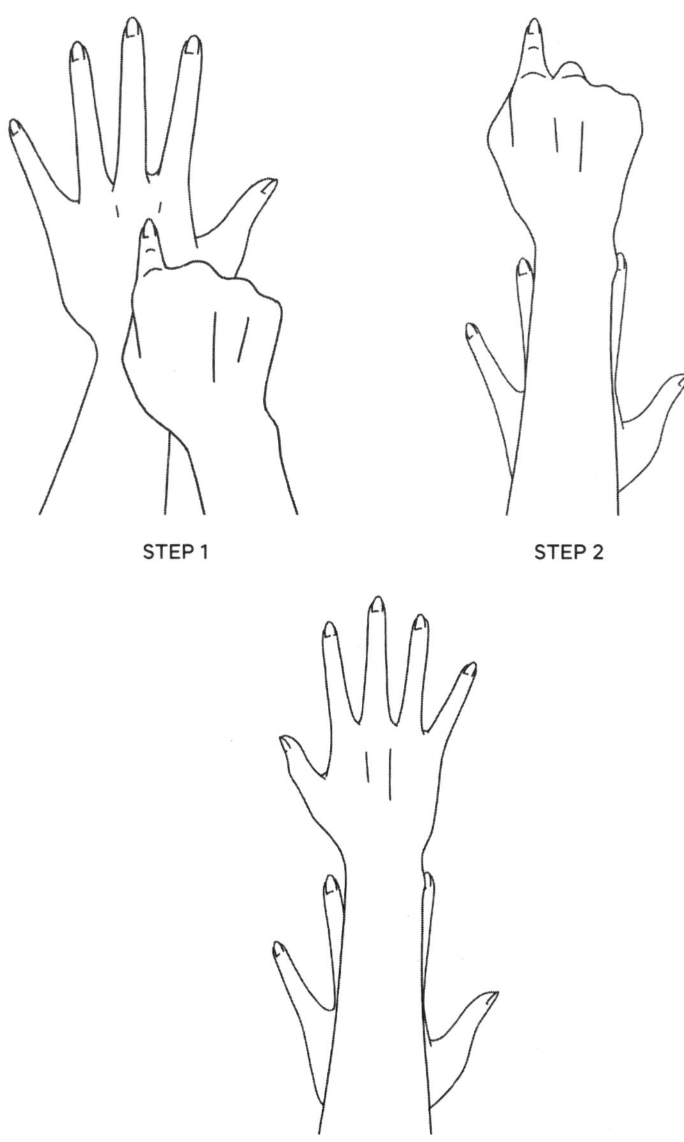

STEP 1
STEP 2
STEP 3

goal. Furthermore, looking at success was simpler than I'd thought. The following exercise is a way to help reframe those moments of frustration and "idleness" when it seems that what you are doing is a failure.

First, extend your left hand as demonstrated in step 1 on the previous page. Think of it as a microcosm of life. Your right-hand index finger represents yourself. You are standing on that path, and in front of you, you have five fingers that spread out as life's possible journeys.

Which finger shall I go down? Shall I go this way? Or that way? Most people fail to pass the second joint of the first finger they chose. They go back and forth, not confident that they have made the best or the right decision. They stand at a central point in their lives and waste precious time worrying. They only need to go a little bit farther to get to the end of the finger path they have chosen, but the majority never make it "a little bit" farther and reverse track. They think they've made the wrong choice, suddenly sure it wasn't the right path for them, even though they never finished the journey to find out. Their destination was just one more joint away at the end of their finger.

Pick a line and follow it to the end, as in step 2. It doesn't take long. When you reach your wrist, stretch your right hand as in step 3.

Can you see? You've made one step forward. Now you know you just need to go "a little bit" farther. It is time to push through now and make it until the end, whatever road you choose. A new road begins. Switch hands again. This time, it is your left index finger that stands for yourself. Open your right hand and repeat steps 1 through 3. You have taken another step. Switch hands again and repeat. That's life. Little steps add up to make a path and complete an entire life.

It's already a victory if you take one foot off the ground, and it's a success if you take even a small step forward. Once you put one foot down, you raise the other off the ground until you reach the end of whichever path you are on. Keep internalizing experiences of success more often, even if they don't seem like much, and those memories will quickly replace the memories of past failures.

Once I learned this useful exercise, I started consciously repeating those hand gestures every time I felt stuck. They helped me move forward, little by little, as my mentor had shown me. I remind myself of those motions when I need to reassure myself about the path I am taking, if I'm going in the right direction, whether I'm moving forward. I've found comfort in this exercise when I feel overwhelmed by anxiety. I wasn't the only one. I've taught it to many people who have come to see me, who have experienced similar emotions, and this small series of gestures has helped them, too.

"So this is what success feels like."

"I feel like I have lived every day to the fullest."
"It's become a habit now."

People who confessed to feeling lost and like they were lagging behind found peace and composure by doing the exercise. It is a powerful three-second reminder that our paths are built by many small steps. Each one is a small success, but you must stick with each step once you start to take it.

A friend who used to have a short fuse and was quick to give up on things said practicing the hand gestures even changed his approach to investing. He called to tell me the happy news that he had made huge profits by patiently holding on to some stocks that, before learning the exercise, he would have given away too early after questioning whether buying them had been the right decision. When I heard his story, I felt sure the exercise had found its way to someone who really needed it. It is an effective method that allows your mind to envision success within three seconds.

Another day, another chance to practice. I make one small step after the other, one hand at a time. I set a new direction for each new day. As you keep practicing, there comes a point when you finally realize: *I'm making progress.*

Keep moving to the tip of your fingers, without giving in to doubt, and you will reach your destination before you know it. When you have no idea where you are in life, or when you're curious how much more you have to go, get a little taste of success with the tip of your fingers. All the successful past steps you have taken will act as momentum and a magnet for the future luck you ardently wish for.

> When I was young and free and my imagination
> had no limits,
> I dreamed of changing the world.
> As I grew older and wiser,
> I discovered the world would not change,
> so I shortened my sights somewhat
> and decided to change only my country.
>
> But it, too, seemed immovable.
>
> As I grew into my twilight years, in one last
> desperate attempt,
> I settled for changing only my family, those closest
> to me,
> but alas, they would have none of it.
>
> And now as I lie on my deathbed, I suddenly
> realize:
> If I had only changed myself first,
> then by example, I would have changed my family.
>
> From their inspiration and encouragement,
> I would then have been able to better my country,

and, who knows, I may have even changed the
world.

—Author unknown

These are the words engraved on a tombstone in West-minster Abbey. The bishop the grave belongs to is no longer part of this world, but he left an important lesson. He teaches us that there is nothing in this life you can achieve by simply snapping your fingers. You can only do your best in every endeavor, and perhaps you will someday find that all those past efforts form themselves into future success.

We all have things we worry and feel anxious about. And most of us aren't brave enough to put our trust in something as unpredictable as the world we live in. Life is already challenging enough without constantly carrying all our troubles, worries, and anxieties on our shoulders. You must try to take lighthearted steps on the path that you have chosen, and do not burden your steps with either negative or positive thoughts. Those efforts you make will eventually come back to you. That's what the saying "All luck begins from yourself" means.

YOUR DISPOSITION ACCORDING TO YOUR ENERGY

Below are some short descriptions of the five energy types. There are websites where you can enter your birth date to discover your Five Elements energy. Try searching for "how to use your birth date to discover your Five Elements energy." Once you know your energy type, you can use the Five Energies theory to attract wealth, success, and money. Further reading will help you understand your energy type in greater depth.

FIRE (火)

* Byeong-hwa, "Fire of Yang" (丙火): You shine brightly like the sun, and you are known to attract people. Your warmth and outgoing personality are good assets in any environment where you get to interact with other people.

* Jeong-hwa, "Fire of Yin" (丁火): Similar to a candle's light, you have a concentrated, focused disposition that draws other people's attention. You would benefit from a career in the arts, because you thrive when you are the focus of the spotlight, like a candle's flame.

WATER (水)

* Im-soo, "Water of Yang" (壬水): You are wide like the ocean. You are an active person who values ideas and originality. Big business would suit you better than restricting yourself to one small specialty.

- Gye-soo, "Water of Yin" (癸水): You resemble cold rain, in that you can be difficult for others to read. You tend to keep your own counsel and can think quickly on your feet. It is recommended that you choose a practical path over which you can have a good amount of control, like being self-employed.

WOOD (木)

- Gab-mok, "Wood of Yang" (甲木): You spread wide like a large tree with long branches. You have the qualities of a leader and tend to pursue honor, which makes you a good politician or professor.

- Eul-mok, "Wood of Yin" (乙木): You are like a small and delicate tree. You are shrewd and quick to understand people and situations. Because you are a skilled communicator, counseling or psychology can be a good fit for you.

METAL (金)

- Gyeong-geum, "Metal of Yang" (庚金): You are steadfast like a rock. You have strong convictions and a great sense of judgment. You will do well in public service, working in a prosecutor's office or on a police force.

* Shin-geum, "Metal of Yin" (辛金): You are a gemstone or metal in polished form. As a perfectionist, you will thrive in a profession that requires delicate and precise work.

EARTH (土)

* Mu-toh, "Earth of Yang" (戊土): You are a vast stretch of land. You are able to coordinate and mediate everything, which makes you a good fit for international work, trading, or brokering.

* Gi-toh, "Earth of Yin" (己土): Damp earth best represents your image. Down to earth and pragmatic, you are well suited for life in society. In fact, working within an organization or being part of a group will be of great benefit to you.

The Psychology of
RELATIONSHIPS

5

Does Money Like Selfish People?

ONE FATE, TWO DIFFERENT FORTUNES

Some people ask, "If I was meant to be rich, shouldn't my life look different than it does now?"

In Korea, a simple internet search informs you of the saju of any famous CEO. Underneath that information, you will always find comments from people who say they were born on the same day and same time as the CEO and, therefore, should also be rich.

In the theory of saju, people born at the same day and time should be living the same kind of life. Of course, in practice, many people are born at the same time as certain celebrities yet never even come close to becoming as rich or successful as their birthday twins. Most of the time, people who share the same saju lead wildly different lives. Just look at twins. Twins spend nine months in the same womb, yet in most cases, their personalities and preferences couldn't be more different.

It is easy to object to the mysteries of saju, so I have been curious to investigate it. Is fate defined in advance? If two people born at the same time have completely different fates, what shapes their fortunes in life? If it is not saju—or not only saju—then what is it?

———

Let's imagine there are two kids. Let's call them James and Jamie. These two children were born on the same day, at the same time. They even have similar names. Both James and Jamie are free-spirited, which makes them a better fit for a life abroad than in Korea. Being trained in languages could also help them achieve great success because they were born with remarkable talent in that area.

James started studying abroad when he was young, because his parents could afford it. Thanks to his exceptional language skills, he is now a renowned international lawyer who speaks five languages. James gained even more recognition as a writer after his book about his success story became a bestseller.

Jamie, however, grew up in a different environment. Born in an ordinary household, he couldn't afford studying abroad and had to stick to basic-level education at school. Thanks to his good grades and his position at the top of his class, he was fortunate enough to be accepted into a local national university. Nonetheless, his responsibility as the eldest son must have weighed on him. Jamie knew he needed to start earning money as soon as he could rather than prolong his studies. That's why he started working right out of school and made a name for himself in the local college entrance exam tutoring industry as a private tutor.

James's and Jamie's lives could not be more different, although both individuals were born at exactly the same time. One achieved success as an international lawyer; the other as a private tutor. I am not trying to compare the two cases and point out one that's better than the other. Still, one can't help but notice that James and Jamie live their lives on different scales. What could be the reason? Innate talent means nothing if you're not given the opportunity to exercise it. That's where lives take diverging paths.

The key here is "special relations"—the people who most influence your life. It can be your parents when you're young, or your partner once you become an adult. That's what makes so much of a difference, even if you were born with the same fate as another person.

Parents' roles are especially crucial during childhood. No matter how much you want to follow your own intuition, you won't be able to do anything about it if your parents hold you back. Parents make most decisions for you, from your infancy through your early childhood, and even after elementary school. Parents make up our whole world, our entire universe, which naturally makes their impact on our lives incredibly significant.

————•

There is one question I often hear: "So you won't have any worries as long as you've got rich parents, right?"

That is not necessarily true. Let's imagine another pair of children, Charlie and Dominic. They were also born on the same day, at the same time. They were both charismatic, enjoyed being the center of attention, and were good at showcasing their talents.

Charlie grew up near a famous talent agency. He naturally developed an interest in the entertainment industry while commuting to school and back every day. One day, by chance, he was recruited by a talent agent who had spotted him in the neighborhood. Charlie made his debut before he reached the age of twenty. Already, he had found his element. On stage, he was as happy as a fish in water. He was a natural-born pop idol. A young man of great talent and ability, Charlie had found his calling and was lucky enough to have encountered the opportunity to realize his fate. He was pleased about how his life had turned out.

Dominic, on the other hand, grew up in a family of lawyers. Whether it was money or connections, he never lacked material support. However, Dominic's parents strongly disapproved of his dream to be in the entertainment business. Dominic grew up hearing criticism such as, "What? The entertainment industry? How did we get an alien like that in our family?!" He eventually went to law school, as his parents wanted, but he failed the bar exam and became an accountant instead. Even while working as an accountant, Dominic's strong desire for a different kind of life never died. Whenever he couldn't contain his irrepressible talent, Dominic would run to a karaoke club to blow off some steam. Deep inside, his unrealized desire to get on stage, to appear on television was still causing him pain.

If your parents ignore your innate potential, like Dominic's did, the silver spoon in your mouth is of no use. We have a special relationship with the first people we meet in our lives. Everyone grows up in a different family environment or atmosphere, to parents with diverse capabilities and worldviews, which leads to unique outcomes.

Of course, some people manage to shape their lives the way they see fit, no matter how great the impact of their parents. You can change your life by deciding yourself what your fate will be. That's free will. Special relations like one's parents have a certain amount of influence on one's life, but they never have the power to completely disrupt or spoil one's fate. In fact, I've discovered that many of the self-made had less-than-ideal parents.

If you think you are unlucky with the parents you have,

and that that will stop you from ever succeeding, then that's as far as you will ever go. On the contrary, if you see your unfortunate family environment as a crucible through which you will forge your strength, chances are, things will turn out well. A certain amount of hardship is essential for anyone to become resilient and be able to endure the adversities of adult life. Of course, you are bound to be affected by your parents or your environment, but you need to let go of the idea that those factors dictate your entire life.

So take a careful look at your life. Who are the special people in yours that impact you? Who are the ones who recognize your potential? If you can think of even one name, you are blessed with greater luck than you will ever realize. That said, don't worry if there isn't a person like that. Sure, life might be easier if there was someone you could follow, but even if there is not, it's not a big deal. In the end, realizing that you are your own savior is the fastest way to attract good luck. Your own faith in your potential is what matters most.

THE SECRET OF WOMEN
WHO MARRY GOOD MEN

"Why am I having such a hard time with relationships? It's not like I'm asking for the moon!"

Attractive and charming, Elsa was highly popular, and her friends envied that about her. She dated men who had everything going for them: looks, background, career—you name it. People who knew Elsa all said she had "a lot of luck with men," but Elsa thought differently.

"I always attract weird guys. The absolute worst even!"

She was actually right. Plenty of men liked her, but none of them had sincere feelings for her or loved her consistently. Men bombarded her with endless material favors, from high-end jewelry to romantic gestures. But once they started dating, they showed their true colors. They would cheat. They would keep multiple relationships going in secret. One even asked her to lend him money. Nonetheless, Elsa had no respite in her love life. Breakups were only temporary. As soon as one relationship ended, she would start a new one. Of course, this was possible because she had an endless line of suitors.

Was Elsa really "lucky" when it came to men? Many people say the more dating experience you have, the better your chances of marrying a good person. That may be true, of course. At the very least, you get a better-trained "eye for people." However, that is no guarantee of a good marriage. Dating and getting married are two completely different things.

You see it often in the world of celebrities: a star who seems to make the right choices and married a perfect match admits a year later that they had been deceived into a marriage that turned out to be very unhappy. Again, being experienced in dating or celebrated in the public world in no way guarantees a successful marriage.

So what does "luck in relationships" really mean? In the world of fortune-telling, there is a very clear distinction between luck in relationships and luck in marriage.

To have "relationship luck" means you are destined to encounter a lot of people. The Korean proverb "fate is in a grazed collar" refers to how easy it is to make connections with people who just pass you by. It means you have a lot of opportunities to meet new, diverse people, and you draw attention wherever you go. You will indeed meet many people, but this is different from finding a good spouse.

People who have good "marriage luck" may not have good dating experiences, "luck in relationships," or many opportunities to meet potential dates, but they get married to a good person without too many complications. In short, when it comes to "relationship luck" and "marriage luck," it is perfectly possible to have one but not the other.

Then what defines the "good person" I mentioned earlier? The first thing most people probably think of is someone who is "eligible" in the eyes of society. I have often noticed, however, that such criteria don't apply to everyone.

—•—

Everybody said it was a great match. She was an ordinary office worker; he was a dentist. They first met as patient and doctor, when she came to the clinic to get her wisdom teeth removed. The woman was not necessarily looking for "good husband material." After their wedding, everyone thought she had managed to marry "a catch," but she didn't see things that way. She was proud of the career she had worked so hard for. She didn't see the marriage in the same positive light others did.

"Wow, a dentist husband!"

"Your life will be a bed of roses now!"

"All that's left for you now is to quit your job and enjoy life, right?"

No one believed her when she told them she had married for love, no matter how many times she said it. She had fallen in love with a person who just happened to have a well-paid, respectable job, but most people had a deeply prejudiced opinion about her marriage, thinking, *She's laid her hands on a good one.*

A few years later, her husband opened another clinic hundreds of miles away in Busan.[*] The expansion kept him so busy that the woman had to take a leave of absence from her own work to help him. She also had to look the part when accompanying her husband to social events. Her old clothes and bags were gradually replaced, but no matter how luxurious the clothes or how expensive the purses, she wasn't happy. She wanted her own business, too, and she wanted her husband to

---

[*] A port city on the southeast coast of Korea.

support her endeavors rather than the other way around. She missed her career, which she had to put on pause just when she was reaching a peak. Only in her thirties, she was too young to let her degree in design and her experience in the fashion industry go to waste.

As her unhappiness grew, so did her husband's frustration. She had taken time off from work to support him, but she felt bored and stuck staying at home all day. As the weeks went by, their arguments became more frequent. The discord between them eventually seeped through the cracks of their personal lives and affected the outside world. The husband found it difficult to focus on his work at the clinic, and his practice shrank significantly. Ultimately, their marriage ended in failure.

Your partner's luck can change the course of your own luck. The union between the woman and her husband was ill-fated from the start. If she had been the type to feel more at ease playing a supportive role rather than asserting herself to the outside world, their union might have been a match made in heaven. For this woman, however, a man who would have let her run free in open fields would have been a better fit. Her husband was on the other end of the spectrum, completely at odds with what she needed, and the marriage never stood a chance. In this case, the partners' union didn't have a synergistic effect that led to better luck. Far from it. The two spouses actually undermined each other's luck. It makes me think that a successful marriage is one in which two people bring each other good fortune, regardless of education, wealth, or other qualities valued by society. A union that's good for both parties is one that creates synergy, where each one becomes a valuable Gwi-In[*] to the other.

———•———

There was a young couple running a sushi restaurant. Their restaurant was jam-packed with customers every day, and the pair worked together hand in glove. The wife worked in the kitchen and was as skilled as any Japanese sushi chef. With a good-natured face and a friendly personality, the husband was so good at managing the cash register and waiting on the tables by himself that they didn't even need to hire extra help.

Those weren't his only skills. Instead of paying for expensive fish from a local distributor, the husband traveled to Tongyeong[†] and got quality fish directly from the market at a lower price. With great hospitality added to fresh ingredients

---

[*] A gwi (precious, valuable) in (person) is a valuable connection, a person whose presence is important and who has a special meaning in your life.

[†] Tongyeong is a city located in the South Gyeongsang province of Korea, approximately 378 km (235 miles) by car from Seoul. It is known for its robust fishing industry, and the city is a hub for seafood, famous for its oysters, anchovies, and sea squirts.

and wonderful flavors, the sushi restaurant's net profit increased by more than 30 percent as the couple was able to open multiple branches. Word of mouth spread, and their restaurant became so popular that the country's largest department stores reached out to them about opening a new location.

Initially, the wife was running the restaurant on her own, and the husband had joined as a part-time employee. The wife was an excellent cook, but her introverted personality made her ill-adapted to dealing with customers as the host and empresario of the restaurant. By contrast, her husband was a people person, the perfect man for that important job. Each spouse was at the top of their game, and working together, they created a wonderful synergy. The young couple filled each other's gaps and enhanced each other's fortunes. You could certainly say they had "marriage luck" as well as business luck.

The story of NCSOFT* CEO Kim Taekjin is another good example. Kim first started his company with less than one hundred thousand dollars. His company grew after he got married, and the couple started running the business hand in hand. Together, they made decisions that proved beneficial for the company: They dedicated a lot of resources to AI development and became the first domestic video game company to own a professional baseball team.

---

* A South Korean video game company known for creating MMORPGs such as *Lineage* and *Guild Wars*.

This is how crucial it is to meet a person who is a good fit for you. Recognizing such a person can be life-changing. Keep in mind, however, that the result of a positive "alliance" is not necessarily money. A "good marriage," according to society, always implies receiving other people's judgment. But who cares about another person's opinion if the married parties themselves are happy?

For a person who was raised by a single parent, lonely and longing for psychological stability, an ideal partner might be someone who is affectionate and stays by their side, even if they don't make a whole lot of money. On the other hand, a person who is good at increasing their assets may be the most precious partner for someone whose objective is to become rich and who values money above all else. At the end of the day, you should be the only and absolute judge of whether your marriage is a successful one.

There is something I tell every person who says they want to marry a good person:

"If you want to meet someone of value, start by being of value to other people. That is how you can truly succeed in marriage. Don't just think about receiving. Cinderella may be happy about everything she gained, but that doesn't stand true for the prince. That's not a mutual relationship but rather an incompatible one.

"Another thing: You should be the judge of whether a person is a good match for you or not. That's how you can become the sole judge of your marriage, and not let others' judgments interfere."

An alliance that generates synergy for both partners, an encounter of equal value where neither party gains or loses: That's how couples who join their fortunes increase their wealth and success.

DON'T LET OTHER PEOPLE STEAL YOUR ENERGY

In life, it is often people who bring you fortune, and people who bring you money. Now that you can meet anyone in the whole wide world, everybody is obsessed with networking. Those who believe "the more the merrier" will indiscriminately save any new number they come across, while others who think it best to keep only useful connections manage them by tier.

But think about it for a second. Does the amount of assistance you've received correspond to the number of people you know? Do the people you've invested the most time and effort in actually help you with a similar effort in return?

The person who saves you the day you collapse on the street will probably be a stranger you've never met before. It is also unknown strangers who offer comfort and a helping hand to those struck by a disaster.

As we go through life, it is more common for luck to come to us through unexpected connections than through the ones we already have. We call it "luck." Then what is the origin of the luck that brings us those precious connections?

———

A construction company executive, Jake had been pouring all of his energy into winning a contract for an apartment reconstruction project. Jake told me he had been working on it for days. He was venting to me about feeling stuck.

"I have a feeling it's going to take just a little more effort . . ."

"This project seems to be causing you a lot of worries," I said.

"Yes, our company is counting on this project as if its survival depends on it, but we're just not making any progress. I feel like we're on the verge of something big, but this client is so fickle, we have no idea what to expect."

Jake's face darkened as he finished his story. I wanted to help him. It was not just the company's fate that was at stake, but the livelihoods of all of its employees as well.

Jake was obviously deeply troubled. He kept scrolling through the calendar on his phone, counting down the days to his next appointment with his client.

Quietly, I made a comment.

"It seems like you're doing the best you can."

"Hmm?"

"You seem so invested in him."

"Yes. I must close this deal, by whatever means possible."

According to Jake, his company was not the only one bidding for the project. Several other construction companies were courting the same client. At first, the potential client had seemed to be leaning toward Jake's company; but lately, Jake had heard that he had been frequently meeting with another company. Jake felt like he was watching his chance to win the contract slip away. I had no silver-bullet solution to offer him when it sounded like the scale had tipped in the competitor's favor. Instead, I gave Jake a piece of advice that I thought might help him get his company back on its feet:

"You must conserve your energy going forward."

"What do you mean?"

"Most people do not recognize the person who is going to bring them good luck. That's why they dedicate their efforts to random people. To try to cultivate a relationship with an ulterior motive makes it even more draining, as you are expecting something in return for your actions. Nevertheless, you must remember you can't dedicate the same amount of energy to everyone around you; otherwise, you will be drained of all of your strength.

"A certain amount of effort is necessary, but you can't channel all your energy toward relationships. Moderation is of the essence. It requires a lot of energy to hope for something, to have expectations. The emotional damage you feel when you experience disappointment in someone's behavior toward you is consequential. It can end a relationship that would have lasted years and years. So just make sure not to push yourself too much in this case."

"Understood. I will try."

I advised Jake to temper his engagement with his client and instead, to treat everyone who reached out to his company fairly, without any agenda or ulterior motive.

Jake estimated that his business had six months left to succeed unless he was able to greatly increase the business income. He took my advice and started interacting with his customers without questioning his own performance or thinking how much money he could make from them. He answered every question with kindness, no matter how small the job, no matter how small the possibility of signing an actual deal. He dealt with everyone as evenhandedly as he could. Thoughtful, kind behavior came effortlessly once he stopped mentally overexerting himself by worrying about the future of his company and everything else. His stress levels decreased, too, because he was no longer bending over backward to satisfy everyone in hopes that it would help his company survive. Surprisingly, he discovered that he no longer felt disappointed a consulting session didn't end in a contract when he entered it with zero expectations.

Still, he always showed his gratitude toward the customers who had traveled far to come see him. The modest projects he secured here and there kept the company afloat for a while. One day, an elderly gentleman in his sixties came into the office, dressed in a battered overcoat. Judging by his attire, it seemed unlikely Jake would win a contract from him. Nonetheless, with a smile on his face, Jake offered him a cup of coffee. The old man introduced himself as a former real estate agent and casually asked a few questions about the costs of moving a shop's location. When Jake walked him through the cost of the construction work, the old man was surprised.

He threw up his hands and said the cost was too high. It was as Jake had expected. The consulting session had gone on for more than half an hour. Perhaps the old man felt sorry for taking up so much of Jake's time. As he left the office, the old man said to Jake, "I'm so sorry, but maybe I can introduce you to someone I know."

Jake walked him out, smiled, and told him not to worry about it.

A few days later, Jake got a visit from one of the gentleman's acquaintances. It turned out he was a well-known property owner in the area who had several townhouses and residential buildings. All of a sudden, Jake's company found itself in charge of a multimillion-dollar construction contract for an entire housing complex.

The redevelopment contract he'd worked so hard to land went to another company that spent every effort wooing the difficult client. From Jake's perspective, however, he was the real winner, because he had won an equally lucrative contract by simply putting on a friendly face and working from a peaceful mindset.

———

You often hear people say things like, "I've been badly betrayed," "I don't think I can trust anyone ever again," or "How could they do something like that to me when I've been so good to them?" especially in relation to money, particularly in matters of investment or business.

But you should stop and think for a second when you hear yourself say such a thing. Haven't you gotten ahead of yourself? Whenever you put effort into a relationship with another person, it requires you to spend a good deal of energy, and all of that effort may end up being a waste if that person doesn't react the way you want them to. You need to always remain aware of whom you are spending your energy on and accept that you do not have control over how they will respond to your effort.

For many years, my father (who is now deceased) received a card sent by his car dealer around the holidays. My father was only one of the dealer's many customers, and he had not purchased a car from him in many years. That dealer had been taking care of his customers in that same way for decades. It felt old-fashioned, like something from the days when people sent handwritten letters.

That said, the dealer's holiday card didn't have much content. It contained a single line, saying "I wish you a great year ahead, and may your days always be filled with happiness." It was a generic greeting, and at first it looked like the dealer had made little effort. But when I looked at the signature, I could see he had made a real effort: The signature was distinctive, carefully and clearly written by hand with great care.

Whenever my father bought something, he would look after it carefully so he rarely needed to replace what he bought. He didn't spend much money on repairs after buying that car, but the dealer kept sending his regards even though he didn't get any more business from my father in the decade after he bought the car.

About one hundred thousand miles later, it was time for my father to buy a new car. He contacted the dealer we all thought he had forgotten about. The dealer had had no hopes or expectations regarding my father. He was just managing his relationship with him, just like he did with all of his other clients. Then a former customer—my father—whom he had not anticipated, called with the good news that he wanted to buy a car from him.

Good fortune rarely comes from someone you expect. More often than not, it comes from somewhere completely unforeseen. This is why it is best to moderate the amount of energy you put into people. Protect your emotional energy, and don't be too generous or too restrained. An unexpected connection will often bring you good fortune if you approach the world without hidden motives.

THE EXPIRATION DATE OF THE GWI-IN

Human relationships can be subject to trends. Even someone who seemed like a benefactor to me can become my enemy after a certain period, and an enemy can become a benefactor, depending on the time. People are also subject to the forces of the time they live in. Sometimes a relationship can be good, and sometimes bad. Some relationships are meant to last, and some are going to end eventually. Recognizing when a relationship is a positive or a negative and when to cultivate or end it can be an important part of managing one's fortune. I was able to witness the dramatic beginnings and the ends of many such relationships ("periodic ties" as I call them).

———

It was early summer. Leonard, a businessman in his fifties, was preparing for the upcoming local elections. Next to him was Philip, his best friend of thirty years. The two had met as young college students at a local university, and their friendship had continued after graduation as they became fully functional members of society.

Leonard got a job at a renowned electronic parts manufacturer, and Philip started working in a small trading company. The pair of them were like soulmates, each compensating for what the other lacked. They became neighbors in a small town, and their friendship grew stronger as they got older.

As Leonard was about to retire, he made a proposal to Philip. He suggested they start a business together, using the knowledge and experience they had each acquired from working at their respective companies. Philip agreed readily, thinking it would be a new chapter of his life.

Philip and Leonard worked well together in business, too. In truth, Leonard had always had a secret dream: becoming a local politician. He hoped that once their business took off, he could enter politics and present himself as the image of a successful entrepreneur.

Leonard's life motto had always been "I can do it," and he certainly lived up to it. His drive was unrivaled. With the best minds in technology and sales working together, the company was soon able to generate an annual revenue of ten million dollars. When the company's profits stabilized and it felt strongly established, Leonard resigned as CEO and revealed his long-held dream of entering politics. Philip applauded his friend's decision. His support was so wholehearted, it almost felt as if they were running for office together.

In the run-up to the election, Leonard was surrounded by a lot of noise, both inside and outside the company. The media had discovered dirt on him, including stories of embezzlement and bribery, and Leonard's name was constantly in the press. Unfortunately, the public connected Leonard to Philip, and the connection put the business they'd built together in jeopardy. Of the various accusations leveled against Leonard, there were many that Philip had not been aware of. Philip was pulled in and out of the police station, having to fight to clear his name. The company's stocks plummeted before the investigation was even complete.

What had been a lifelong, highly fortunate friendship had completely changed. It was difficult for Philip to maintain his friendship with Leonard after he learned about his wrongdoings. "To forgive or not to forgive?" In the end, Philip decided to cut ties with his old friend, not only for his sake, but also for the survival and stability of their company.

Leonard subsequently suffered a major defeat in the election. Philip felt bad about it, but in the end, he felt he had made the right decision. What if he had let himself be taken hostage by his friendship and been dragged down by their severely damaged relationship? The whole company could have been jeopardized, and rebuilding trust between them would have been difficult.

The embezzlement charges against Philip were finally dropped. Philip was able to get out of a sticky situation by ending a tainted relationship, and the company recovered, too.

———•

This story is not only about the damaged friendship between Philip and Leonard. Ultimately, their relationship had an expiration date, which took them decades to reach. For years, they never knew how far apart their values were from each other. Leonard, who had been exposed for embezzlement and bribery, and Philip, who had led a righteous life, were on two completely different life paths. It was only when Leonard's secrets were exposed and Philip saw the immense gap between their values that he realized he must cut ties with Leonard, even if they had been college friends, neighbors, and business colleagues for so many years. If a relationship no longer serves you, if it has reached the end of its life, it is better to put a stop to it as soon as you recognize it is no longer serving you.

The same goes for romantic relationships.

A couple both had job interviews and helped each other prepare. She got the job; he didn't. They still loved each other, but the young man kept voicing his anger and frustration at being rejected, and he soon fell into depression. At first, his girlfriend tried to comfort him and cheer him up, but his depression didn't show any signs of abating.

Over time, his feeling of depression turned into an inferiority complex. Deep rifts developed between them. The topics of their conversations changed. They had longer and more heated arguments every time they saw each other.

If you can support each other through tough times, everything is likely to be okay. But if you can't bridge that gap and it starts affecting each of your lives, your relationship likely has an expiration date. If you find yourself spending more than 60 percent of your time together arguing, it's a sign that the relationship has reached its end and you really must consider whether it is worth continuing to be in it.

Whether it be with parents, friends, or colleagues, there is a Gwi-In for every period in your life. When your time with a certain Gwi-In ends, you have to let that relationship go to make room for another. Through new encounters—and new Gwi-Ins—you progress through life.

DISTRIBUTE FAVORS; COLLECT PAIN

Yoo Jaeseok is a Korean TV host who is admired by everyone. Many people look up to Yoo, calling him their role model. His generosity is always beyond what any ordinary person could ever be capable of. He helped a younger colleague in need with a large financial contribution to their wedding, and he makes sure that the underdogs who appear on his show get enough screen time. He is adored by the entire country and is in high demand. The rumors that he has many millions' worth of assets are probably not exaggerations.

Singer-songwriter IU is no different. Every year during the holiday season, she sends gifts to everyone she has collaborated with. The heartwarming stories from people who are touched to receive her gifts spread across the internet and the airwaves and show how much she values relationships.

It almost seems as if the stories of celebrities' good deeds are the key ingredient in their recipe for success. The good actions themselves may not be the exact reason, but in the end, their stories highlight something about successful people I have noticed in my work: They often seem to reciprocate the love they receive by taking care of those around them. As a result, many of us give them our adoring support and take inspiration from their words and actions.

Some people may be inspired to think, *I should give more*, or *I should be more like them and be more generous.* Certainly, there is a portion of luck that is heightened by the act of giving to others. However, I have also seen in my work that that doesn't mean you should always be generous. Sometimes, instead of making your life better, being generous can make it worse.

———

"I don't seem able to save any money. It's so strange. I don't even spend that much."

I had a friend, Stella, who always complained that she was broke all the time in comparison to her colleague, who would be all smiles because she had savings that were growing. They both got paid the same amount on the same day every month. It didn't even seem like Stella had a particularly extravagant lifestyle. *Why doesn't she ever have money?* I wondered.

Not long after, I figured out why Stella was struggling. Her problem was other people and how she related to them.

Stella was a natural giver. She would never hesitate to treat the people around her to a big meal when she was in the mood, and she always gave birthday presents to friends and family members. If anyone she knew got a promotion, moved, graduated, or got admitted to a school, she never missed the opportunity to send them a congratulatory gift. She also spoiled her boyfriend with luxury wallets, clothes, and cosmetics for every anniversary.

By contrast, Stella was extremely stingy with the money she spent on herself. Instead of buying books, she only read the pages she needed to while standing in the store. Instead of buying cosmetics, she only used the free samples she got from promotional events.

Stella's problem was that all of her spending faced outward, toward others, rather than to herself. No wonder she never had any money, because she gave it all away to other people. Of course, there isn't a problem if that made her happy, but Stella was constantly complaining that her hard-earned money was disappearing. I told her that her "excessive generosity" was problematic.

The reason why the beloved TV host I mentioned earlier gives thousands of dollars for someone's wedding is not because he's famous. It's because he's rich. Imagine if an ordinary office worker like Stella, who earns two thousand dollars per month, contributed such huge amounts at every wedding she was invited to. She would be on the streets, penniless, before she could even be praised for her generosity. What if, instead of spending all of that money on others, she had invested it for herself, and consequently became rich and successful? She could probably be as generous as she wanted, without always complaining about the state of her bank account.

My point is not that you should be tightfisted or refrain from giving to others. I'm saying you should always keep in mind that there is an order of priority, even when it comes to giving. If you want to attract good fortune, spend money appropriately, choosing the things and people you spend it on wisely and never forgetting to prioritize yourself first—at least until you are very wealthy and can afford to prioritize others!

Microsoft founder Bill Gates announced his intention to give away almost all of his $200 billion fortune. For decades, he has donated to a wide range of causes, including climate change, poverty alleviation, etc. The active way he has donated since becoming a billionaire is further proof that he has achieved the perfect balance of wealth. He invested in himself first until he became wealthy, then began giving back.

In short, wealthy people are well aware of how to invest, when to harvest, and when to give. This is something that the nationwide popular TV host and the top singer mentioned earlier have in common.

Even now, there are people around us who give tirelessly, although they themselves are in great need. Have you seen any of these people become rich? Chances are, you haven't. On the flip side, you can easily find examples of people who give generously after they have become rich. Because they have already achieved a certain level of success, those people are able to give freely, regardless of the circumstance.

There is an unspoken part of the phrase "sharing brings blessings" that really should be at the start of the quote, and that is, "When you have a lot." Take a look at people who don't hesitate to buy meals or coffees for others but spend little on themselves. You will notice that they are also miserly with their time and money when it comes to their own learning and skills acquisition. It is highly unlikely that a person who doesn't invest healthily in themselves will ever become one of the "happy few" to join the ranks of the wealthy and successful.

When you don't have a lot, sharing doesn't always make you feel blessed or happy. On the contrary, it often makes your life harder. It's never too late to give back after you have reached a comfortable position. If you try to spread your own luck and wealth too widely to others before you've used it well for yourself, you may end up with no luck for yourself. Luck, unlike money, cannot be divided into smaller pieces.

In conclusion, if you are determined to become rich, give to yourself first. If you've got money to spare, invest in yourself first. That's the fastest way to save money and accumulate wealth.

HIDE YOUR STRENGTH; BIDE YOUR TIME

"If you want to make your dream come true, spread the word as widely as possible."

This is advice you often encounter in self-help books. People tell you the more earnest your desire, the more you should let everyone around you know. Those self-help books say it doesn't matter if you tell people your dream in speech or in writing. They say just be sure to communicate it loudly enough that word will reach a Gwi-In, who will come and help you. Even if it doesn't happen immediately, your luck will take a turn for the better thanks to some unexpected event that these self-help authors say will happen because you told the world about your dreams and ambitions.

Is this true, though? Is it necessarily wise to so easily reveal your cherished dream to a world that may be untrustworthy, when you have been holding on to it for so long?

———•

A group of friends have been together since childhood. Let's call them Noah, Taylor, and Victor. Noah and Taylor work at a small company and don't have any specific dreams they want to realize. Victor, on the other hand, always wanted to become rich. He was constantly on the lookout for an opportunity to get a foot inside the entertainment industry.

His energy was better suited for a dynamic job than a static, office job. He wanted to work as a celebrity manager because he had a lively personality and enjoyed interacting with people.

Victor was still in his twenties, which meant he had his whole life in front of him. He talked about his dream openly with his two friends. But every time he did, instead of receiving support, he was met with ridicule.

"A manager? You? Come on."

Rather than helping him figure out how to make his dream a reality, they trashed the job, arguing it was the type of job that would never take him anywhere.

"Managers get paid so little," said Noah.

"I hear they don't even get time off on weekends," said Taylor.

These pronouncements were not based on any firsthand knowledge. Noah and Taylor were just repeating negative things they'd heard from others about being an entertainment industry manager.

Constantly hearing Noah's and Taylor's negative comments discouraged Victor. He questioned his dream constantly, wondering, *Is this the right path?* and *Am I wasting my time?* His best friends, far from being helpful, were actually hindrances. Victor grew more disappointed and discouraged by the day.

Yet he didn't give up on his dream. He decided to keep his mouth shut until he made his dream come true.

"The time has not come yet. I shall hide my intentions for now."

As soon as the new year started, Victor moved to Seoul. One by one, he knocked on the door of every entertainment agency until one of them gave him minor tasks, such as assisting a talent manager or a casting director. He wanted to gain direct experience, so he talked his way into managing a singer who was just starting their career. It was his first real management job.

Up until then, Victor hadn't told his friends what he was doing; he kept his big dreams for the future a secret. He didn't want to be undermined by his friends' negativity and interference.

Victor built his career step by step. He was diligent and so well liked that he began working with stars everybody knew by name. As his career in the industry grew, his salary skyrocketed. He was especially admired for his ability to nurture and maintain long-lasting relationships. He kept in touch with actors, cheered them on, and looked after them even once they left the agency at the end of their contract. The celebrities he worked with could not help but be impressed by Victor's work ethic.

Finally, Victor used the years of trust and the reputation he had built to open his own entertainment agency. To begin, he only managed a couple of entertainers. However, the strong bonds he had formed kept attracting people to him, regardless of the contract fee. The entertainers who were being managed by Victor with so much care and support also saw their luck and good fortune grow. Soon Victor had become the CEO of a top entertainment company with sales in the hundreds of thousands of dollars. Now that he has achieved his dream, Victor talks to his friends about his dream freely and proudly.

—•—

People are less interested in your dreams or goals than you might think. They're all busy living their own lives. In other words, the people around you are not equipped to, or don't have the bandwidth to, supply you with the crucial information that will help you succeed. Even if they were in possession of such information, they seldom feel the need or have the willingness to share it with you. There is nothing surprising about that, because it is normal for everyone to put themselves first. No matter how much you talk about your future aspirations, there is a limit to the useful information you will get from the people around you.

Thankfully, we are living in a time when anybody can easily obtain or verify most of the information they are looking for online. That makes it unnecessary to reveal the details of what you want to achieve to other people. Talking too much about your dreams can have a negative impact, exposing you to being the subject of gossip, unwarranted meddling, or nagging, which will lower your morale. People often speak too lightly about things that are actually none of their business. In my own experience, other people's advice is more often unhelpful, and sometimes completely useless.

And let's not forget about envy. It's a problem in every interest, although in my experience, it is particularly intense in the entertainment industry. Since entertainers' survival depends on luck and popularity, rare are the ones who can tolerate seeing others do well.

For these reasons, it is sometimes necessary to follow the Chinese proverb, "Hide your strength, bide your time (韜光養晦, Tāo guāng yǎng huì)." Don't easily reveal your deepest thoughts. Instead, build up your skills, and seize what you want when the time is right.

Cover your light just a little bit. Strong sunlight can blind you and prevent you from seeing where you're going. It can make you resent the warmth that you normally enjoy. The same rule applies to human relationships. Talents and ambitions that stick out too much will often earn you hatred and resentment, and those could easily become thorns in your side as you work your way to good fortune and success.

In conclusion, it is often best to conceal your desire to accomplish something until it becomes 90 percent certain that you will indeed reach your objective. Being too vocal about your dreams can cause all of your good luck to disappear. Ultimately, the people around you can sometimes help you in small ways, but you are the one who needs to take action.

So don't tell, just show. The wealthy all know how to surreptitiously mask their true feelings.

Write your Intentions in Cypher.
The passions are the gates of the soul.

The most practical knowledge consists in disguising
  them.
He that plays with cards exposed runs a risk of
  losing the stakes.
The reserve of caution should combat the curiosity
  of inquirers:
When your opponent sees into your reasoning like
  a lynx,
conceal your thoughts like an inky cuttlefish.
Do not even let your tastes be known,
lest others utilise them either by running counter
  to them or by flattering them.

—Baltasar Gracián, Spanish philosopher

YOU HAVE TO GET LUCK TO GET MORE LUCK

What brings you good luck? What brings you money? From my perspective, it's always people. As humans, we are not meant to live alone. Even if two people spend the same amount of effort under the exact same conditions, the results will be widely divergent based on the encounters with other people they make along their way. If you think about it, we all have different attitudes depending on whom we connect and interact with in life.

There are people who are blessed with great luck for relationships, people who move forward thanks to a helping hand that always seems to appear to them in the form of a person whenever they're in need, no matter where they are going. We say that they have good "people luck." There was a day when I crossed paths again with just such a person in my own life, and it underlined to me the importance of people luck.

———•———

In the winter of 2012, I opened a café in Gangnam while I was still in college. It wasn't something I had started on a whim. I wanted to make a lot of money, and I wanted to spend money in a better way.

Everything was going incredibly well, considering it was my first time ever running a business. As the monthly sales steadily increased, my school attendance got worse. I started getting more ambitious for the business, imagining I could make a fortune if I kept opening more stores. I even contemplated quitting school and changing career paths altogether. Then one day, someone suddenly appeared in front of me and blocked my way. It was one of my professors from the program I was enrolled in who was training me to become a producer in the entertainment business.

"You can do business at forty-five. You should make the choices that are appropriate for your age. That's the wiser way to live in this world."

"I don't think so, professor. I've already made up my mind."

"You can't be a producer after twenty-five. Come back to school and get the training you need before it's too late."

"I've already made my decision. I don't think it'll change."

"But you've only taken one step into the business world. Trust me; come back and let's try again. What do you say?"

"But . . . Okay, I'll think about it."

Even after that inconclusive exchange, the professor continued to come find me at the café. I was stubborn and unwilling to give up. Additionally, the success rate for the broadcasting exams—and the jobs available if you even managed to pass—were a thousand to one. I took it as a sign that I should not try to become a producer. I didn't want to go back to the reality of my university courses.

The professor visited me three times. If they had stopped coming after the second time, I would have gone all-in on the business of making money, and I never would have become a producer. Looking back now, I realize they were the type of lucky person for me that I will probably never meet again in my life. At the time, however, I was just bewildered, not understanding why they were trying so hard to convince me to complete my media studies. The school was packed with students trying to get into the broadcasting industry; why did they bother with a student who had already left school?

Many years later, I couldn't contain my curiosity and asked the professor directly.

"Professor, why did you tell me to come back to school?"

"You really want to know?"

"Yes, I want to understand why you came all the way there to see me . . ."

"Because I have a lot of luck with people."

"What do you mean?"

The story my benefactor told me that day was very intriguing. The professor told me that during the past several decades, they had had a few strange encounters where someone would appear and help them move forward at just the right time. The professor gave credit for this lucky, timely help to their "luck with people"; without that help, they were sure they would have not progressed as far in life as they had.

"I started my broadcasting career in the provinces at first. I didn't have good luck with exams, and without great results, there was no hope of starting my broadcasting career in Seoul. Like today, even then, getting a job in broadcasting in Seoul was very difficult for a new graduate. But one day, I got a call from a senior producer working in Seoul. They asked me to come to Seoul but didn't give me any explanation for why they had tracked me down. I had a million things to do at my job, but I went to see them anyway. It turned out the producer had gotten me an interview for a career producer position in the entertainment department. I passed the interview and immediately moved to Seoul to work. That senior producer was, in fact, my Gwi-In."

The professor's story continued. The miraculous connections didn't stop there.

"That wasn't all. I met wonderful colleagues and cast members who believed in me and followed my lead willingly. Thanks to that, every entertainment program I worked on became a huge hit. Time went by, and before I knew it, I got older. In broadcasting, producers often find their shows moved to less-desirable time slots as they age, making me wonder if my best days were behind me.

"But then someone offered me a university professorship. I couldn't believe how good the timing was. So once again, I took the hand that Gwi-In had extended to me. That's what brought me to teach you all. I can't list them all, but there is not a single thing in my life I have achieved without help. Every step I took, I was moving forward holding someone else's hand, then another hand and two steps forward. That's how I moved on in life, step by step. When I look back at it, I think my whole life has been like that."

"That's the reason why you came to see me?"

As I thought about my own life, I realized I had had a similar experience. I had realized my dream of becoming a broadcasting producer by holding on to the hand my professor had extended to me. Then, when I had left the broadcasting world again, someone else had reached out and offered me a job.

"Director Yoo, would you be interested in working with me?"

I had gotten a call from a high-ranking executive at TV Chosun. They had produced the most successful idol program in the country. In the Korean broadcasting industry, everybody knew who they were. For such a high-ranking person to readily offer me a position to start a whole new program was a golden opportunity for me.

At the time, I had just left another station, so I politely declined. Creating a new program felt like a huge mental burden, plus my business was going well, so I was having fun making money.

Only a few months later, I got another call. This time, I stopped everything and went for it. They made an offer I couldn't refuse: I was given free rein to do whatever I wanted. In the broadcasting industry, where seniority was directly related to your age, to be given full authority as a young producer was rare.

———•———

I still hadn't gotten a precise answer from my professor about the real reason why they helped a nobody like me, so I asked them again. A smile spread across their face. The professor told me: "Because I saw your potential. I felt like if I just reached out my hand, you would grab it. I owe my whole life to the people I've met who brought me good luck. That's why I have such strong faith in luck. If you receive help from a person, you should give that same kind of help to someone else. That's how you make good luck come back to you."

That explained it. The professor was building up good

luck. They had already benefited from luck many times from other people, which allowed them to buy a car, purchase a house, and free themselves from financial want.

They knew the joy that their help could bring to someone else's life better than anyone. They couldn't ignore the good fortune they had cultivated and that they had been given. So whenever they had the chance, they scattered seeds of help, good luck, and good fortune here and there, feeling thankful for any chance to reap the fruits in return.

But they didn't go around offering help to any random person. They only did so to those who knew to grab the hand they were extending. In a certain light, they were being generous and giving. At the same time, their determination to pass on luck to others to increase their own was thoroughly centered around themselves.

It was a probability game of sorts. The professor had experienced both sides of the exchange many times over: helping others after they had gotten help from someone and receiving help from a person they had helped before.

In the end, the people who could be your Gwi-In are people you have already met or will meet in the future. I've learned that those who have helped me or been helped by me are more likely to become a Gwi-In.

Nevertheless, you shouldn't expect the help you give to always come back to you as luck. If it does, good, but it's also fine if it doesn't. Just think of it as planting the excess of luck you have received here and there like seeds. Then, someday, it may come back to you. Life is something that can't be complete without someone's help or care.

This is how successful people harvest good luck. They are open to being given a hand and prepared to give a hand, always aware that good and bad luck can crop up at any time, so planting luck and reaping it whenever it appears can help overcome the inevitable times of bad luck. To them, people are money; people are seeds.

HOW TO RECOGNIZE YOUR GWI-IN

Rich people do not allow just anyone into their circle. They are ruthlessly selective about who they do business with or who they marry. They do so because they know the monumental impact a person can have on their fortune. The fact that frequency videos have been gaining traction in recent days, gathering millions of views, is not unrelated.

Just like radio waves or sound waves, every person has a unique frequency. Our frequency is low when we feel at peace, and it increases when we get excited. We cannot help being affected by other people to some degree, just like the way trees sway when the wind blows. That includes a romantic partner, a spouse, a colleague, a business partner, or a friend. Consequently, meeting a Gwi-In can, by itself, offset a lot of bad luck. It can also make a huge difference in your life.

Incidentally, it's actually pretty simple to find a Gwi-In. Share a meal together. The act of eating is highly valued in the world of fortune. In the olden days, food was scarce, so making a living was the most pressing issue. Based on the science of Myeongli, to have good fortune for food was linked to wealth and abundance. Therefore, the act of eating food with another person became a symbol of invaluable blessings and an occasion to evaluate each other's energy in the most direct way.

Some people increase your appetite and raise your spirits just by eating with you, while others make you lose your appetite and cause your energy levels to drop, even with a succulent meal in front of you. Furthermore, there are some people you can eat with comfortably, while with others, you somehow feel uneasy the whole time. As you can see, sharing food with a person provides you with a context in which you can quickly assess their energy and its impact on you.

So if you want to know whether someone is a Gwi-In, eat together. That's the reason why, in the moments leading up to a business meeting or a date, we bring up the topic of food: "Let's have a meal sometime."

The Psychology of
EMOTIONS

6

How Not to Get Crushed by the Wheel of Fate

WHY ARE WEALTHY FAMILIES ALWAYS HIT BY TRAGEDY?

One day, a friend of mine who worked at a major newspaper told me something that left me dumbfounded. Working in broadcasting, I had heard about so many incidents and mishaps that I didn't bat my eye at most news. This time, it was different. A tragedy had hit a very wealthy family. It felt like "trouble in paradise," as if torment had penetrated a sacred land ruled only by prosperity and peace.

"You know the president of XX Group? His son died yesterday."

"Just like that? What happened?"

"I heard it was suicide."

"Are you serious? What could have gotten into him? He was from such a wealthy family . . ."

"It's under wraps for now. We got a call from the group last night. They asked us not to make it public until they're done with the funerals. The decision has been made, so everybody's keeping it quiet."

"My goodness, I can't believe it."

"Me neither. I guess money isn't everything."

The family of a prominent entrepreneur had lost their son. They said it happened while the young man was studying abroad, but the exact circumstances and cause of death were unclear. People were making all kinds of assumptions, wondering whether he had gotten into drugs at parties or wound up in a mess after associating with the wrong sorts of people. Unsubstantiated rumors circulated everywhere.

"Do they know why he did it?"

"Who knows? Nobody's talking."

"Hey, why do you think tragedy constantly strikes wealthy families?"

"They don't realize how lucky they are. Isn't that what they said in that drama? If there is one thing that someone who's too poor has in common with someone who's too rich, it's that life feels boring to both of them. I've never been that rich, so I wouldn't know. Anyway, it looks like money doesn't necessarily bring you happiness. So rich and yet so miserable . . ."

Can having too much money cause problems? Does it mean that it's better to be a down-to-earth, ordinary person than to be inconceivably rich? The more money you have, the happier you must be, obviously.

As I thought about this story, I realized there was one thing I was mistaken about: the nature of money itself.

———•———

Whether they are conscious of it or not, the public is always curious about the wealthy. To be born with a silver spoon in your mouth is considered the greatest luck of all. It's a life that everybody wants, especially these days. You can have anything you want when you're rich—cars, luxury goods, the future. In short, being rich is a blessing, a gift from heaven.

But stop for a second and think about it. Whether it be chaebols in Korea or the so-called "mega-rich" in other countries, these families regularly suffer the loss of a child. A little research will tell you that many prominent entrepreneurs or chaebols have gone through that kind of tragedy. It doesn't end there, as you'll also find suicide attempts and public scandals involving drugs or drunk driving. On top of that, discord among family members, divorce, and inheritance disputes constantly disturb their peace. Tragedies big and small keep happening to these families, even though the public is mostly unaware of them.

How can you explain that chaebol families are constantly hit by tragedies? Why does it seem like fate never leaves them alone? I have asked myself similar questions countless times since I have entered the world of luck. I wanted to find the root of the problem. I wanted to find the pieces of fate that bound them like a bridle, fit them together one by one, and come to a satisfying answer that would clarify everything once and for all. Not long after, I reached a point where I felt like I had finally found the key to solving that long-standing enigma: karma.

Children are born with the genes their parents have passed down to them. These genes contain a variety of information about the parent, influenced by the environment they grew up in, their education level, and the economic support they got from their parents, suggesting inheritances of intelligence, emotional resilience, and bodily health. The child has no say in deciding whether they want to receive those genes, but they must continuously ride this mental and material "flow of cause and effect"—their mental, physical, and emotional inheritance—as they navigate through life. That's karma. The heirs of chaebol families in particular inherit a large amount of resources and wealth, and that includes the karma of the family money.

Depending on the case, money has good karma and bad karma. Children can be punished for the bad karma their parents have accrued, or they can be rewarded for their good karma. More often than not, it's the former. Money being a product of human desire and will, the karma associated with it comes with much heavier consequences.

———

The man in front of me looked like something was troubling him the entire time we met. He was the chairman of a pharmaceutical company he founded when he was twenty-eight. His company had developed a cold medicine that proved so effective, it became a household name throughout the country and made his fortune. His company was now a well-established medium-sized business that recorded three hundred million dollars in annual sales, and it seemed like everything was going well for it and for him. Nevertheless, as you get older, you are bound to face one or two issues that cause you trouble but that you might feel you cannot share with other people.

"I have no child to pass my company down to."

Born in a slum, the chairman worked as a delivery boy during the day and went to school at night. He was the textbook case of a successful self-made man. From his thirties until his sixties, he dedicated every waking hour to developing new medicines and managing his company. He never took a day off, nor did he have any hobbies. All he did was work, work, work—and make money. He later went public and made a name for himself as an entrepreneur. Having built such an impressive company from scratch, he was looking forward to the relief and peace of mind he would find after he retired. He imagined himself enjoying old age after having entrusted the company to his children. Sadly, that was wishful thinking.

His children did not share his thoughts in the least. To them, the chairman was an absent father, always so tied up with work he barely ever spent time with his family. He had not even attended his son's graduation. His children saw the chairman as a fundamentally unhappy person. They vowed to themselves, "I will never be like my father."

The man had sacrificed his entire life to build his company, only to be ignored by his children. His children, on the other hand, had never won their father's approval despite doing their best. Naturally, a conflict broke out between the parents, who had to pass down the company, and the children, who wanted nothing to do with it.

———

People say, "First-generation chaebols flourish and succeed; the second generation deserves praise for even managing to stay afloat; but the third generation inevitably encounters crisis." The first generation in other words, the founder—grows fast because they are obsessed with success and don't give up easily. These qualities, however, are lacking in the second and third generations, who never had to overcome the same level of difficulties as the founder. The second and third generations suffer unexpected pressure and pain because their parents expect their children and grandchildren to preserve what they have built. That's what causes all the conflicts and antagonisms among the generations. This can all develop into great unhappiness if they don't manage to resolve those differences.

In the end, having more money than you can handle is a curse. It lures you toward illness, drugs, scandals, suicide, and other traps of fate. A family is considered lucky if that sort of unhappiness happens to only one person. In some cases, it brings down the whole company or shakes up the very foundation of the household. The scale of the disaster is usually proportional to the amount of money the family possesses.

That is the reality of the unresolved karma of money, the karmic burden that gets passed down to the next generation. All things considered, it may be better to be a reasonably rich person than to be born into extravagant wealth.

Eventually, the pharmaceutical company fell under the responsibility of the chairman's eldest son, who took over against his will. It goes without saying that the young chairman was met with considerable opposition from the elderly executives.

Being born into an affluent chaebol family triggers a lot of envy, but the chairman's eldest son felt as though all happiness had been taken away from him. He had not just inherited his father's company, but also the responsibility for the livelihoods of hundreds of employees, along with the pressure to maintain the family assets and grow the business even further.

Karma can be likened to a vehicle that only moves forward and never stops. The anger, anxiety, and oppression that come with money were part of the inheritance the chairman had bequeathed his eldest.

THE SEVENTH ENEMY OF LUCK

Does saying you're lucky actually make you lucky? I have seen many self-help books that conveyed a message along these lines. Of course, auto-suggestion could work, but becoming lucky is not so quick and simple. It's not something you can achieve through words alone. Telling yourself, *I will have better luck* is not a guarantee that you will. If you are as familiar with luck as I am, you know that is a fact that's not going to change.

Then what about the opposite? What if somebody else said you were going to be lucky? All of my clients I tell this to show the same reaction. It made them feel so happy to be told that there was light at the end of the tunnel. They were like children who had just been given candies. They all said, excitedly:

"I promise to work hard from now on!"

"That gives me so much strength. I'll do my best!"

But only a few actually put their words into action. Knowing the future one step in advance can also have a significant side effect.

———

A friend of a friend, let's call him Nick, was working in the financial district of Yeouido[*] and doing quite well for himself. Nick was an investment banker who was planning to retire when he reached his forties. He wanted to keep making money after he stopped working in trading. After careful consideration, he decided to start a business.

Perhaps because he was an experienced financier, he was knowledgeable in economic matters and had a flair for business. He first dove into the coffee industry. Exchange rates were still stable then, and the domestic market was fairly dynamic as well, which created a favorable environment for him to start his business.

Nick imported coffee beans from countries like Brazil, Colombia, and Ethiopia, and sold them at reasonable prices. He worked hard, determined to lead the coffee market. Of course, he was under a lot of pressure. The thought of losing the one hundred thousand dollars he had initially invested in his business kept him awake at night.

---

[*] A small river island in Seoul that is the equivalent of the City in London or Wall Street in New York.

Nonetheless, things were looking good for Nick. When I accidentally bumped into him one day, I gave him some casual words of advice. I sensed he was about to have an unexpected stroke of luck, and I was hoping he would take advantage of it.

"Next year is going to be a good year for business."

Nick went home with a twinkle of hope in his eye.

————

For about a month, it really did seem like things were improving. Nick felt much more at peace. Even his insomnia got better. Unfortunately, he was overlooking something crucial. Before our conversation, Nick was spending 80 percent of his time worrying, only making concrete efforts during the remaining 20 percent. Knowing he was about to have better luck, he could spend less time worrying about his business and take meaningful action instead.

A couple of domestic companies were already starting to dominate the market, which should have prompted Nick to do everything in his power to promote his products—distributing samples to individual café owners, for example, at the very least. Alas, Nick put all of his trust in luck and stopped making an effort altogether.

As Nick became less preoccupied with his business, he started dating. His business was nowhere near stable, but Nick started seeing women and spending time drinking with his friends. He also indulged in some expensive hobbies he had been putting off. He had one justification: "She said business was going to be good next year."

———•———

Three months passed. Nick had gained weight and was drinking more. He was wasting his 80 percent in meaningless ways. One day, I ran into him and asked him: "Is something the matter? How should I put this . . . You seem so leisurely, so laid-back."

He answered, with an air of unconcerned indifference, that he was working on it, telling me he was talking with a potential client who was about to open a seven-thousand-square-foot café in Paju, Gyeonggi-do.[*]

Nick's answer took me aback. It couldn't be more obvious that, in its current state, Nick's company was going to fall behind in the market. Even at that very moment, his competitors were working day and night, battling aggressively against each other to secure more clients, targeting large cafés that were proliferating rapidly in the suburbs. Nick's excitement about his "successful deal" when he didn't even have a piece of paper in his hands looked nothing short of foolish.

---

[*] Paju is a city located on the northwest side of Seoul, in the Gyeonggi-do region.

I realized then I had made a grave mistake. I should not have meddled in another person's fate so indiscreetly. Master Kang Heon, a former music critic turned Myeongli scientist, is known to spend no less than three days analyzing one person's fortune. That is how difficult it is to assess a human life. Fortune is not a field to be treated lightly, a simple concept that can be appraised with just eight letters. But I . . . I had succumbed to my "good intentions," my desire to wish Nick well, and let myself heedlessly intervene in his life.

"Ah . . . Luck is real, but it's all meaningless if you don't understand human nature."

Most people will start to relax upon hearing they will have better luck. They often suddenly decide to make up for everything they denied themselves while they had been working toward their current goals.

Some may say, "You need time for your personal enjoyment, too," and that's perfectly valid. However, Nick had had a clear business objective in mind, and to achieve that, timing was of the essence. If he wanted to expand his business, he needed to secure a solid client base instead of spending all of his time dating and drinking.

That's the reason why I sometimes tell people not to rely too much on the luck that they're given. If you've got time to relax and wait for luck to "do its magic," I tell them it is much wiser to actively work toward your goal. Hearing or learning that your luck is going to improve can bring you some peace of mind, at least in the short term. However, if you're not careful, you can become complacent and ruin your fortune with your own doing. It is no wonder that sloth is one of the seven deadly sins.

In the end, Nick wasted half a year "waiting." The owner of the large café in Paju he was "having good talks with" ultimately chose to work with a competitor who was offering lower prices than Nick. Nick did nothing but wait for a windfall, twiddling his thumbs, and he paid the price.

If only Nick had come to his senses before the exchange rates shot up. If only he had dedicated the extra time he gained to his new endeavor. Then maybe Nick's business would have taken off, riding the wind of luck. Sadly, Nick's sloth was his biggest enemy, and it blocked his road to success.

PEOPLE WHO SUCCEED NO MATTER WHAT

"With five hundred thousand dollars in annual income, I should be rich in five years!"

David was a researcher in the heavy manufacturing industry. He had studied abroad at an engineering school and gotten a job at a corporation as soon as he got his degree. When asked about his dream, he would invariably respond: to become vice president of a company. Although he started from the bottom, David was ready to do everything it takes to climb to the top. It was the greatest result he could achieve as an ordinary man.

Passionate about everything, David had a better foundation

to start from than his peers who had stayed in Korea for their studies. His foreign degree earned him a relatively high starting salary, thanks to which he was able to accumulate some savings. His parents, approaching their seventies, could not have been prouder of him. But perhaps he did not know how to stop. David's eagerness to become rich gave rise to imprudent ideas for generating extra income.

David started investing in Bitcoin while he was working at his corporate job. Every night, he spent hours watching YouTube videos about investment on his phone, dreaming of the day he would tell the world about his wildly successful investing adventures. He didn't stop there. He started using the little knowledge he had to give palmistry classes through an online platform, going so far as to collect payment for his "lectures."

The more he focused on his side job, the less attentive he became to his main job. He even started planning his online classes during office hours. He got busier and busier, planning his schedule down to the minute. Nevertheless, all that extra side work wasn't turning into the everlasting stream of income like he expected.

Fast-forward five years. David was still a low-level employee, moving from one company to another. He was passed over for promotions due to his poor performance, and kept changing jobs within his field. All the while, he kept telling people:

"I don't understand why I never get a promotion. I work so hard!"

"I've tried everything I could think of to make money. Why am I still poor?"

If he had focused on his main job and delivered good results or invested his time and effort in networking within the company, David would have gotten those promotions or at least learned some information about them beforehand. Instead, he was getting further away from his dream of becoming vice president, chasing two birds that were each going in a different direction.

Although there is nothing wrong with wanting to be rich, you won't be able to avoid making mistakes if you rush the process and think about raking in the money before you're even ready.

A bangjja yugi[*] that has been hammered several thousand times in a thirteen-hundred-degree fire has nothing in common with a plastic bowl that comes out of an injection mold at the rate of four a second. The two objects may look relatively similar, but put some food in them, and you will realize that it doesn't taste the same, nor does food last nearly as long in a plastic container.

The same goes for money. You can put as much money as

---

[*] A bangjja yugi is a type of traditional Korean bronzeware. It was often used by royalty because of its sterilization and antipathogenic properties.

you want in a container, but if the container has no durability, it's not going to last. Money held in an unstable vessel can spill and spoil anytime.

———•

More people become rich in their later years than you might think. That was the case for a lot of my clients, including a head of the family in his fifties. He had lived in poverty for many years after his children were born and belatedly started a small business selling speakers and amplifiers, which he grew into a profitable medium-sized company.

When people hear such stories from me, they just feel relieved. They think, *Oh, they were late bloomers*, or *Success found them late*. The assumption behind such reactions is that it was thanks to coincidence that those people succeeded, that they "got lucky." That is nonsense. People just don't become that wealthy overnight. Perhaps the expression "a healthy seed leaf"[*] would be more appropriate, in the sense that these people should have achieved success even earlier.

The rules of life mandate that nobody can become successful if they haven't done anything to deserve it, no matter how

---

[*] From the Korean expression, "You can recognize a tree that is going to grow large and healthy even as a seed leaf."

long they wait. Nobody. There is something that people who became rich late never fail to say: "I wouldn't have gotten where I am today if I hadn't struggled as much as I did."

Curiously, some people take it as a self-comforting, "I'm not rich now, but I will be some day," kind of statement. That's just wishful thinking that opportunity will find them despite them not putting in their best effort to reach their objective.

This is why I tell people that the desire to become rich quickly won't help them if they are destined to be late bloomers. Perhaps this is a good moment to revisit the meaning of the expression "Great talent blooms late." I sometimes tell people this phrase to remind them that some dreams take a long time to make happen. But I also tell them, whether I sense they will be a late bloomer or not: "People who are bound to succeed, succeed no matter what."

That's the kind of people they are.

THE GREATEST FORTUNE COMES AFTER THE GREATEST MISFORTUNE

I doubt there is anybody in this world who considers themselves lucky 365 days a year. Even the luckiest of us go through challenging moments.

The first time it happens, people think: *Oh well, too bad, but that's okay.*

The second time, they start having doubts: *Hmm . . . I keep getting unlucky.*

When it happens again, people start thinking differently: *Ah . . . Maybe things are not meant to happen for me.*

And when they get defeated repeatedly, they give up: *I knew it . . . I'll never amount to anything.*

When you constantly feel like life is beating you up, you become frustrated and lose hope. Next, you start emanating a dark, negative energy that drives people away. You keep failing and grow increasingly hopeless. A vicious cycle begins. When your luck dips, especially in a crucial period like your twenties, it ends up affecting your personality. It can literally transform your destiny.

Once something like that happens, you become unable to seize luck even if it comes knocking at your door later on. Even at times when money and opportunity are there for you to grab, somehow, you seem unable to grab what's right in front of you. However, don't despair even if that's the case. Life is like a river; just because you missed something once when it flowed by doesn't mean you can't grab the next thing that does.

Life always has its ups and downs, so when you experience a setback, be wise enough not to absorb all of the emotional impact. Rather, be resilient enough to use that shock to spring back up. Think of it as a roulette game, where instead of letting the marble run loose, you use the obstacles and edges to make it bounce back.

As Tom sat in front of me, I noticed it took him a while to steady his shaking hands. For seven years, Tom had been the youngest head chef at a five-star hotel, cooking food and making desserts without a moment's respite. But his early success had fueled a lot of jealousy from envious coworkers. He had to endure ruthless finger-pointing every time he turned his back. After seven years, he left the hotel. He was planning to open his own dessert shop using everything he had learned working in the hotel industry.

For the time being, however, he confessed he needed some rest before he could put his plan into motion, which I didn't find surprising. I couldn't leave Tom standing at a crossroads like that, so I quietly told him, "It's okay to take some time before starting your business, but you need to pull yourself out of your current emotional state."

"What do you mean?"

"Sand pits are dangerous because the more you dig, the more the sand shifts downward, increasing your risk of being trapped.

"Emotions are the same. If you stay buried in your emotions without resisting, you will end up destroying yourself. Do you think taking one or two years off will give you the confidence you lack? On the contrary, it will probably wipe out any certainty you have. You will be afraid to start a new business, and you will forget everything you learned while you continuously hesitate and put things off. When your luck takes a turn for the worse, you don't stay there and absorb the shock; you do your best to remove yourself from that bad place so you don't get swept away."

I was right. Tom was a perfectionist, the kind who would knock on stone bridges before crossing them. He was also a highly sensitive person with a delicate, snowflake-like personality. He admitted he couldn't even look at an icing knife without his heart racing.

Tom was getting more and more depressed as he thought back to the exhausting and traumatic relationships at his previous workplace. Even if Tom did start a dessert shop, someone as introverted and shy as him would need at least six months to promote the shop effectively, and a year until the business reached a point of stability. Was he strong enough to endure such a long period of uncertainty? It is difficult for most people to get out of an emotional sand pit, but it was especially true for people like Tom.

I gave him one final piece of advice: "Do something that doesn't bring you any money. It can be anything."

Usually, it is better not to start anything when you're going through a bad phase because no matter what you do, you don't get any results. Tom's case was different. He had to do something, even something small, to avoid being submerged in his emotions.

Tom agreed, nodding. Then he began to take steps toward independence.

He needed to find something that didn't yield any immediate financial results but still kept him moving. He first focused on getting a sugarcraft qualification. It was an essential technique to master if he wanted to start a dessert business.

A few months later, Tom opened a luxury dessert shop in a prime location on Dosan-daero[*] in Gangnam. He went for a high-end boutique concept with a high price point, thanks to which his revenue reached seventy thousand dollars a month. He is doing so well that he is expanding his business, getting ready to open a second and third location. Tom said he no longer has the impression of being in a bottomless pit and feels much lighter now.

"I'm not captive to my emotions anymore. I feel like I could do anything. I have stopped being afraid of my old coworkers, or the icing knife."

Depression makes you feel like you're trapped in the sand. Once you let your feelings dominate you, nothing goes right, whether you have good luck or bad luck. Even money passes you by. That's because negative energy chases away any incoming luck.

———•———

For a while, the phrase "depression is water-soluble" was trending on social media. Internet users were arguing that

---

[*] The area around Dosan-daero is a popular luxury shopping destination, also recognized for its trendy restaurants and cafés, cosmetic surgery clinics, and high-end residential buildings. A Western equivalent would be Fifth Avenue, New York.

feeling better after a shower was proof that water washed away the depression.

Does it, though? According to a study conducted by psychiatrists, working out and going for walks are the only activities that are scientifically proven to be effective against depression.

Tom's example convinced me of one thing: "Depression causes atrophy" is a more precise way to describe depression than it being water-soluble. Digging into your depressive thoughts will make you feel overwhelmed and powerless, as if you were being swallowed by sand. If you leave your negative feelings alone, on the other hand, they will gradually disappear. Getting away from those negative feelings will put your luck back on an ascending path: You can reverse its course by refusing to let your emotions bury you.

In the end, only those who have control over their emotions can ride their luck upward and take command over their fortune and wealth. Once you've fallen into depression, it becomes difficult to motivate yourself to do anything. However, nothing is going to change if you just lie in bed feeling down. That's why you must start working on something as soon as possible to shake off those negative feelings.

The accomplished hotel chef no longer fears what his former colleagues think of him. He doesn't regret leaving or the interruption in his career. The mere fact that he has freed himself from the shackles of his own emotions has made him a rich man. You can see that his greatest happiness was waiting for him at the end of his greatest misfortune.

THE LAST CLIENT

Winter had already arrived at the foot of Mount Bukhan. I got up in the early morning hours and put a fresh bowl of ok-soo[*] on the altar. I always start my day by cleansing my mind as the sun rises.

I opened the heavy iron door of my house and stepped into the garden, with its lush trees and mountain stream, surrounded by ancient brick walls. A pine cone that was barely hanging on its branch the day before had fallen to the ground. The wind or a squirrel must have knocked it off.

"Something must have pushed it off the branch."

It was always so fascinating to witness the various natural phenomenas driven by invisible forces. It reminded me of the cycle of luck.

In a way, I found it somewhat ironic that someone like me, who had frolicked in the material world of fame and popularity, was now reading fortunes in the spiritual world that

---

[*] Literally "jade water" or jeong-hwa-soo, which indicates the freshest and cleanest water of the day drawn from a well at dawn. It is one of the most basic and essential offerings to the gods.

controls wealth and fate. On the other hand, I was conscious of the fact that this, too, was a choice I was destined to make. Another day had begun, leading yet another life to my door through the sinuous hills of Pyeongchang-dong.

———•

"Ms. Yoo, I can't find any meaning in life."

The old lady in front of me introduced herself as a former designer. She was also the older sister of a veteran actor. She immediately struck me as a remarkably distinguished person.

In her mid-seventies, she looked more like an aristocrat than an ordinary grandmother, with her gray hair neatly coiffed into a stylish bun. Her thick, flowy silk Hermès scarf and luxurious handmade oversized shawl were enough to convince me she was tremendously wealthy.

The old lady slowly started to speak. Her story was quite interesting.

Her husband had passed away many years ago. Her children lived in the United States and traveled every year to see her. Playing golf from time to time with her friends was her only pastime. She had enough money for the rest of her life. She didn't have any special interest in material things, nor did she have any particular worries. If there was one thing she wished for, it was to pass down her massive fortune to her grandchildren without too many complications. Yet she said that life felt unbearably boring to her.

Looking at her, the old lady seemed so dignified she almost came across as lonely. She continued with her story.

"To tell you the truth . . . I have nothing to do. You may not understand. I don't mean to say I'm lonely or unhappy, just that life doesn't excite me anymore. I have been there, done that. I have had everything. I have been to all the places people call paradise on Earth. Now every place looks the same, wherever I go. I no longer find anything stimulating in life. I even find it difficult to feel emotions like joy or sadness. I'm literally just breathing. Having nothing that interests you means that you have nothing to live for."

Her eldest daughter was a brilliant woman who had graduated from law school in the United States, married a Korean-American businessman, and founded a happy family. Her youngest daughter was also very bright. She had gotten a bachelor's degree at a Korean university before being accepted to the Parsons School of Design, one of the top three fashion schools in the world. She was now beginning her career as a global designer with those degrees under her belt.

The lady's younger sister also had a happy life. She had built a solid, decades-long acting career and was as beloved as ever. The old lady and her sister had always been close to each other, and the two sisters loved each other dearly. Her children as well as her sister could not have been more successful. Her entire life seemed filled with success.

Yet the old lady objected, stating flatly that her family members' lives were theirs and had nothing to do with her.

"How could you not be happy with so much wealth?"

I couldn't understand.

"When I was young, I did wonder how nice it would be to have a lot of money. That was especially true when I was working as a designer. I was so preoccupied with chasing money and success at the time. I launched my first brand three years after I made my debut as a fashion designer. I even realized my dream of expanding to the United States. As I gained more and more celebrity clients, I got more orders for haute couture pieces. I made so much money so fast. Money was no longer a concern, wherever I went, whatever I did. That's how I've lived for the last forty years. But now that I don't want for anything, I wonder what I could possibly do with my life. That's all I can think about, and I am at a loss. I learned carrying luxury bags and riding in foreign cars only makes you happy for so long. Those things made me excited for two weeks at the most."

Looking into the old lady's empty eyes, I realized.

She's already tasted the biggest excitements she will get, and she knows it.

There was such a great gap between her and ordinary workers who lived from paycheck to paycheck, which I found ironic. Whereas the latter worried about fundamentally realistic things such as, *What can I do to make a living?* or *When will I be able to buy my own house?* the old lady's mind was pondering spiritual questions, like, *Can I say I've had a happy life?* or *What is a fulfilling life?*

———•

I had one fundamental question: How can humans still feel unfulfilled when there are so many things you can do with money?

I have met people from all walks of life before and after I entered the world of luck. Dealing almost exclusively with celebrities and rich people, my standards had been set high. It made me think that wealth was the last key to a complete life, to reach true happiness. I had been mistaken. More often than not, the actual life of a star looked nothing like how it seemed to an outsider, no matter how much they earned.

The moment you hit the summit, the only way is down. That was the very reason why a hardworking comedian broke down and completely disappeared from the public eye right after he reached the top: He had felt an incurable hopelessness at the thought that he "could climb no farther." Some people give up, exhausted, in the middle of their ascent, and some people lose the will to live as soon as they reach their goal.

Extremes always have something in common: Neither side can be happy.

The old lady stared into the void for a moment, then her gaze shifted toward the pine tree on the other side of the window. What she said next surprised me.

"Ms. Yoo. To have something you want to do, something you want to have. That's the best. To desire something worth three thousand dollars when you only have one thousand in your hands. That yearning toward something, the sense of purpose that you have to make money. That's the best you can have. That's what gives you 'the strength to live.' Don't you think? I don't even have that now . . ."

When I stopped to think about it, there was indeed a significant difference between a rich person with no desire and a rich person who still has desire. The former's five senses have been satiated, so there is no such thing as "the next step" for them. On the other hand, the latter is inspired by an inextinguishable thirst toward life because there are still many things they want to experience.

The wealthy who enjoy happiness in their old age are those who retain a sense of reality. They are able to hold two birds simultaneously, spiritual fulfillment and material abundance, by leaving some room to continue to exercise their willpower. They never lose sight of those objectives and spare no effort to continue to realize them, whether it be a precise amount of money or an as-yet unfulfilled dream.

The old lady didn't ask me for a single piece of advice during the whole thirty-minute session. She unwrapped and shared her feeling of bottomless emptiness, then simply left. She was the first and last client to teach me a lesson about wealth and fortune, instead of the usual case where I am the teacher.

She taught me that it's better to have a dream, even a small one, that you believe in, even if it means that your fortune is still to be made. What I learned from the old lady was an invaluable lesson I wouldn't exchange for all the gold in the world.

Now that you've learned the secret of wealth and fate, what kind of rich person should you aim to become?

WHERE THE GODDESS OF FATE DWELLS

Solve one problem and another appears. I found myself in such situations multiple times with clients since I started reading fortunes. I'd help them with one problem only for them to return with another. Then, at some point, I realized something: So many people had trouble letting go of the anxiety caused by a problem they couldn't do anything about.

Few people lose sleep over the question, *What if my boss gives me an assignment tomorrow?* Most people feel anxious about vague problems that they don't need to worry about right away, such as, *Should I keep working for this company?* or *What am I going to do next year to make a living?*

Things are rather similar with luck. Nobody comes to me asking what they can do to make up with their partner after a fight. In most cases, people are curious about the distant future, like, "Is this person a good partner for marriage?" or "Would we be happy together?" With regards to money, people are more focused on areas they can't solve themselves than on concrete, realistic questions such as how much money they are planning to make and how.

———•———

There was a man who lived in a land called "Anxiety" and dreamed of becoming rich. His lifelong conundrum and mission was to figure out where to put his money once he had it. His very first move was to set up a secret account in a Swiss bank to evade taxes. Once he got that done, he encountered another problem. He wondered how he was going to earn the massive amount of money he needed to fill his account. After some thought, the man started doing everything he could think of to make money. He lived frugally all of his life, spending less on essentials like food and clothes.

After many twists, turns, and sacrifices, he managed to save one million dollars. It was time to send his money to Switzerland. But that wasn't the end. People who dreamed of becoming rich, like him, had been sending money there for years. It had gotten to the point where the government had started to take measures against tax evasion by investigating financial matters and asking for nationals to justify their overseas money transfers. Another unexpected variable had come into play. Now all the man worried about was how to send one million dollars to Switzerland. Alas, he died before he could find an answer. He had focused all of his attention on his one million dollars, oblivious of the fact that he was sacrificing his health to save money. He had been so absorbed in trying to protect himself from an uncertain future that he had completely neglected the reality in front of him. He had let his anxiety lead him astray. That's what anxiety does to you.

If your objective is to earn millions, don't just dream about it. Break it down into smaller amounts, and make those your goals so you don't miss your life along the way by chasing one all-consuming, sacrifice-requiring dream. Dream about a reasonable kind of wealth. There is such a thing as luck in this world, just like there is a right time for everything. So don't worry about the invisible forces of luck and timing that you cannot control. Instead, forge your own luck from what is in front of you, so that good fortune and wealth are sure to come your way.

———

"Thank you, that was really good content. I hope we get to work together more often."

A cheerful sound notified me that I had gotten a message. I checked my phone. It was an email from the production crew that had commissioned a program.

Not long ago, I saw a transfer had been made to my bank account that I wasn't expecting. I counted the zeroes following the number one. There were five. One hundred thousand dollars. I had gotten paid the same amount as the people I once put in a completely different category than me. I couldn't believe my eyes.

It was about this time last year that I quit my job. I left the network, but I never stopped broadcasting work. For several months after I went out on my own, I dedicated the entirety of my time to producing content. I was focused on nothing but work, to the point I overlooked transfers into my bank account.

All the while, I established a production company under my own name. I had no intention of neglecting what was once my dream job just because I had moved into the world of luck. As a CP (chief producer), I worked night and day, bending over backward to create good content.

Nothing was easy. I suffered losses after the web drama I had put a fortune into got canceled before it had a chance to shine. After that, I was able to make up for those losses thanks to the entertainment show I had made by integrating the lessons from my previous failure. My company kept growing as I hired new recruits whenever my revenue increased. Gradually, we expanded our business from broadcasting shows to mobile and YouTube content, viral videos, and more.

Here I am now, fully aware of the luck that has come to me. I have witnessed my income increase two hundred times from the five hundred dollars I earned the first month I was working for myself. This dramatic change was also a transition phase: It was time for me to exchange the effort I put into shaping the luck I was given into a golden ticket. As I meditate on this change in my fortune, I can't help but think of an old story about the goddess of fate I had come across in the past.

———

There is a goddess in Roman mythology called Fortuna. She is always shown holding a wheel that she uses to determine a human's fate. This image of the goddess is commonly understood as an allegory that shows how life's beginning and end are determined in advance. The humans clinging to Fortuna's wheel symbolize those whose lives are upended due to the caprice of fate, or they illustrate human life itself, including both its golden ages and its dark ages.

In one of her hands, Fortuna is holding a rudder that she uses to control fate. The wings on her shoes hint at the elusiveness of luck. Finally, she is also equipped with a bottomless jar that depicts a state of unattainable happiness.

One element we should pay attention to is the fact that Fortuna is often portrayed with a globe by her side, which stands for the incompleteness of fate. The globe is used as a device to convey that even a deity cannot always assess human fate, and that one can always change their fate with their willpower.

Now I understand fate and fortune better. If there is no such thing as an immutable destiny, you must create your own. Nobody knows where their fate will take them and through what paths. You can have a vague idea of its direction, as you do with the wind, but eventually, you're the one who has to find out by living it.

I used to ask: *Do I have good luck? Do I have bad luck?* Now I ask myself and gently nudge my clients to ask: *Am I the type of person who waits for luck or creates their own luck?*

A lot has changed since I joined the world of luck. Now I have a broad idea about my own fortune, and I understand that most people have relatively ordinary fates.

At this moment, my past struggles have become blurry memories.

I no longer feel anxious or worried about money. Instead, I do my best to live each day as truthfully as I can, one step at a time. In the end, I'm the one who spins the wheel of life, and the goddess of fate that holds the reins of fortune resides within me.

UNEXPECTED WAYS TO CHANGE YOUR FATE

Career, love, marriage, money, riches, success, honor, longevity . . . What else in life is determined by fate? Some say everything is decided in advance. Those people are only half right. You can change your destiny depending on what you fill yourself with, like the saying, "It's a flower vase if you put flowers in it, and a honey jar if you fill it with honey."

There are people in this world who change their destiny by sculpting and polishing their lives every single day. They have dedicated one thousand hours to this endeavor. The method is actually quite simple.

The first thing these people do when they wake up in the morning is to think about what they need to do that day. You can have a certain level of control over unexpected risks and mistakes if you anticipate what might happen. Planning ahead is the first step to changing your destiny. Let's say you're meeting with a client. You are bound to try harder to make a good impression on them if you have a thoroughly prepared mindset. That sort of approach will probably bring better results as well, as you won't be completely caught off guard in case you have to act off the cuff.

The last thing these people do before they go to bed each night is to reflect critically on what they did that day. This process allows them to refine their destiny and their approach to it and gain command over tomorrow. They compliment themselves on what they did right and give themselves encouragement for what they could do better. They examine where they lacked patience, where they struggled, and so on. Working every day bit by bit to change your destiny gives you control over your heart, too. It's the same reason why an unprepared person will never achieve success, no matter how great their destiny.

Min Ji Yoo is a lifelong student of luck and fate, descended from a long line of Korean mystics. In her twenties she worked in the Korean TV industry, where she observed how successful people harnessed their luck. She draws from her knowledge of Korean traditions and the intuitive gifts she inherited from her grandmother in her work advising clients on attaining wealth in all its forms.

Jinmyung Lee is a conference interpreter and translator who works with English, French, and Korean. She holds an M.A. in International Public Management from Sciences Po Paris and an M.A. in Korean–English Interpretation from Ewha Womans University. She is currently based in Seoul, South Korea.